LOVE LETTERS

LOVE LETTERS

Paul Gambaccini

Michael O'Mara Books Limited

First published in Great Britain in 1996 by
Michael O'Mara Books Limited
9 Lion Yard
Tremadoc Road
London SW4 7NQ

'Scott' was first published in slightly altered form in *Radio
Boy* by Paul Gambaccini, published by Elm Tree Books,
London. Copyright © Type and Talk Establishment

A CIP catalogue record for this book is available from the
British Library

ISBN 1–85479–644–5

1 3 5 7 9 10 8 6 4 2

Designed and typeset by Keystroke, Jacaranda Lodge, Wolverhampton
Printed and bound by Clays Ltd, Bungay, Suffolk

CONTENTS

To David and Terry

INTRODUCTION

I n the mid-1990s, in the dying days of the Tory era, when
everyone from gay military officers to mad cows had
reasons to regret voting Conservative, I realized I had to
do a gay project. One reason was anger. I was fed up with
certain politicians and newspaper publishers using their
positions to propagate prejudice. Whether they personally
were bigots or not did not matter. They used their influence
to encourage British citizens to discriminate against and
disparage homosexuals. If gay men and lesbian women of
future generations remember them at all, it will be to curse
their names. I saw no reason to wait for their deaths:
I could protest while they were still alive.

The other reason I felt compelled to speak was as a
witness. I do not need a professor to tell me I have lived
during an important era in gay history. We have come out;
we have been accepted by the general public; we have been
used as scapegoats for a terrible disease. Through it all, we
have survived as a community, and we are stronger for the
adversity.

I could not immediately figure the right medium in
which to speak. It could not be a play, for I would find it
impossible to resist the temptation to be didactic. 'To be or
not to be' would become 'to be or not to be gay', and horrified theatregoers, first numbed and then appalled by my
speechifying, would walk out on the soliloquies faster than
Robert Stack walked out on Jack Benny's Hamlet in the
original *To Be or Not To Be*.

I also knew my project could not be a novel. I would be lousy at love scenes. Everyone from Melvyn Bragg to Newt Gingrich (and that really is as wide a range as can be imagined) has come in for hoots of derision over their more steamy passages. There is no reason to suppose I would be excepted from the chorus of catcalls. Besides, I would be awkward. Not only don't I use forbidden four-letter words in conversation, I don't even feel comfortable using five-letter words beginning with 'p'.

So my gay project was assigned to that part of my brain which holds future schemes. One day everything would coalesce in my mind and I would know what I had to do. From that day forward, instead of procrastinating, I would be driven to work until I was finished.

So much for self-knowledge. Eventually the project did take shape for me, but, because it was episodic, I experienced great arcs of interest and burn-out. Weeks and in one case months elapsed between chapters.

Hopefully, if you've gotten this far, you've bought the book and are safely at home or in a moving vehicle being driven or piloted by someone other than yourself, and in a few moments you'll discover exactly what does await a couple of pages ahead. But, if you have to be convinced to continue or if you're merely a reader of introductions, I will try to explain what's going on. It took Marvin Gaye a whole album to try to explain what's going on, so I hope you'll at least allow me a few paragraphs.

'Letters.' That was it. Some concept, I hear somebody snort. Wait: 'Letters to people I no longer see'. Well, that makes sense, we all have people we'd like to communicate with but are unable to for various reasons. 'Letters to people I no longer see who represent the full range of my feelings for other men.' Now I was getting excited. This was my project: to write to men I no longer see, for all the reasons you no longer see people, with all the emotions a gay man in my time would have for the other men in his life.

This would be my witness. This would be my gift to the

gay community. It might be returned the next day, like Teenage Mutant Ninja Turtle dolls the year Mighty Morphin Power Rangers were the rage, but at least I would have given what I have to offer. To my dear friends, to my loved ones, to the homosexual men who have staggered with me through the years of Gay Liberation, AIDS, right-wing politics and Pride, to the youngsters who are now coming out with attitude and openness, which we may have helped bring about, but never dared to dream we would see, this is what I can give you. This has been my life.

And these have been among the men I have loved. So this doesn't turn into a one-note samba, I have tried to select people who have played different parts in my life, and I have tried to write about each in a style that corresponds to the emotions they evoke. Alas, Melvyn Bragg and Newt Gingrich fans, there are no steamy scenes. I have let the feelings do the talking. As a matter of fact, only two of the men I have written to were ever lovers of mine.

Which leads to the really sensitive bits. No, not erotica – libel. In the letter to Scott, I write of someone I refer to as Carl: 'This wasn't his real name and there wasn't anybody called Carl in the news department at the time. He may have changed my life then, but I am in no mind to change his now.'

This has been my policy throughout. Names have been changed to protect both the innocent and the guilty if sexually sensitive scenes arise. For example, it will not surprise you on reading the letters to George and Stephen to discover that these are pseudonyms. In fact, to avoid unintentionally embarrassing anyone, I have sometimes also altered the names of cities, the nature of people's employment, and the identities of third parties. Humiliation or revenge is never my intention: to expose my own feelings is.

This does not stem from any neurotic need to purge myself in public. I am not using the reader as an inexpensive therapist. I merely wish to record what it has been like to be a gay man in my time. Most other such works seem to concentrate on the sexual or lifestyle angles. I'll stick to emotions. You will just have to believe me when I tell you that I have not been an athlete in the bedroom, unless the sport be synchronized sleeping. You will certainly believe that I have never affected accoutrements of the day, whether they be long hair, short hair, no hair, moustaches, ear-rings or body rings. You're dealing with a man who lived through the late 1960s without ever once wearing flowers in his hair.

Some names do remain the same, however. Scott, David, Terry and Chris are obviously real people. They are men I have dearly loved without ever being lovers. It would be an insult to their outstanding roles in my life for me to change their names. For David and Terry, the torch I carried has been transmuted by time into an eternal flame, and it is to them I dedicate this book.

HENRY

I loved you long before I knew it. I loved you before I knew what love was and, by the time I knew, you would have forgotten me.

I'm the boy who was your best friend in kindergarten. You probably remember the games we played under Mrs Jacobs' direction. Maybe you remember that, when we had to construct a vehicle from paper, I built a fire engine – why I'll never know. The sides were segmented rectangles of crayon colours, not the usual red, and why I did that I'll never know either. But one thing I came to know, over thirty years later, was that you were the first person I ever knew for whom I had The Vibe.

It's a terribly corny expression, I realize, more redolent of the Beach Boys than the Lover Boys. But just because it's banal doesn't mean it isn't accurate. The Vibe is a tinge of eroticism which is at the heart of all my relationships that contain it. It doesn't necessarily lead to sexual activity, but it charges the atmosphere. The Vibe is all potential, no consummation. When I say I felt The Vibe for you, I mean that my attraction to you was different than to any other boy in the classroom. It meant we had the potential to be important to each other, not only in the ways made possible in conventional friendships but also in the way that separates gay men from straight friends. Assuming, of course, you had The Vibe for me, and this I will never know.

My family moved from the Bronx to Westport, Connecticut, in the winter of 1955, before I finished kindergarten and long before we could have grown into mature friends. It wasn't until I was in my mid-thirties that, upon being reintroduced to a teenage buddy, I recognized what I had felt for him in high school had been a precursor to what

I later felt for my lovers. It was a jolting experience. I felt like blurting out, 'Dick!' (and wouldn't you know it, his real name was Dick) and telling him that, without knowing it, I had really loved him – but who wants to learn twenty years later that someone you had thought was a hale and hearty school friend had secretly sniffed your undies because they had a crush on you? I decided not to tell Dick I had once felt The Vibe for him.

But I am telling you, Henry, and I am telling you because you were the first. Inspired by that close encounter of the nearly gauche kind with Dick, I went through my memory bank of friends, starting with college and going backwards in time. I easily recognized that some friendships in all phases of my life had been characterized by The Vibe. As I delved deeper into my past I was surprised to find The Vibe associated with boys who were my friends even before puberty. I shouldn't have been shocked – not if I feel the attraction between men includes fundamental emotional bonding as well as physical excitement. This tie is part of identity, the exhilarating part that allows us to inadvertently say 'we' or 'us' instead of 'I' and 'me'. So yes, Henry, yes, even in third grade, it was The Vibe for Jimmy and not for Eric, and in first grade, when I was all of six years old, it was The Vibe for Billy and not for Hoyt, and when I was in kindergarten, it was The Vibe for you. It was for you, Henry, and you were the first. You were the first person for whom I felt a foretaste of what would become the most important part of my life. Can you imagine our filmed story? *Homosexuality: The Prequel*!

If you think I'm exaggerating, just take a look at my wall of original comic art. There, among the more famous *Peanuts* by Charles Schulz, *Dick Tracy* by Chester Gould and *Superman* by Curt Swan, are three daily and one Sunday *Henry* by Carl Anderson. The entire quartet of framed pieces dates from 1935. Four is the highest number of originals of a single feature that I own. (Of course, two entire landings in my house are festooned with Donald

Duck and Uncle Scrooge lithographs by Carl Barks, but that is another enthusiasm altogether.) The reason I collected these *Henry*s is that they remind me of you.

You see, I can't remember your real name. I must have known it when I was five years old, but in learning a lot of trivial things since then I've forgotten a few more important ones. What I can remember is that I thought of you as Henry, because you had the shortest haircut of anyone in the class, a real crew cut before anyone had heard the expression 'skinhead', and Henry, a 1930s comic strip character still popular in the newspapers of 1955, was a completely bald child. The other characters didn't seem either to notice or mind this tonsorial tragedy. Nor did I. It was far preferable for me that you be nearly bald like Henry than to have the page-boy styling of Harold Foster's Prince Valiant or the count-'em-on-one-hand long hairs of Charlie Brown.

The other noteworthy thing about Henry was that he never spoke. I don't believe he was medically mute, for two reasons. First of all, this was a mid-century family humour strip. I don't think Carl Anderson, who left the title in the early 1940s, had wished to create a worthy piece about a boy who triumphed over a handicap to take a useful place in society. As a matter of fact, Henry was not very useful: he was useless, being outwitted by various animals when he wasn't scamming his own friends. The second reason I don't think Henry was unable to speak was that, when he was finally given his own comic book, long after Anderson had departed, he was allowed to talk. The mysterious charm that gives a work of fantasy its unique atmosphere was broken, and Henry became just another obnoxious kid, typical except that he had forgotten to grow hair. King Features Syndicate had wisely shut him up again by the time I knew you.

Henry didn't speak. You could, but I can't remember anything you ever said. I remember things we liked, though. Do you remember that we used to collect bus transfers? It sounds improbable now, mainly because one can't imagine a public transport system bothering to be this complicated, but the various buses that worked the Bronx had different coloured passes which enabled passengers to change lines without additional charge. And so, in a warm-up to collecting bottle caps, which was itself preliminary to the serious stuff like baseball cards and comic books, we collected bus transfers. Henry, if you happen to have become a psychiatrist in your adulthood, you might wish to consider that I most fondly remember the pink and orange transfers.

And did you see Robert De Niro drive down our street playing a bus driver in *A Bronx Tale*? In this film, set in our borough during the late 1950s and 1960s, his character earned a living driving a bus, and there on the destination board for the whole world to see was Sedgwick Avenue. I was so excited, so proud, that I told everybody, including Robert De Niro. Poor guy – he was over in London promoting the film and, when I got the chance to interview him, I prefaced our recording with the full quota of the movie's accuracies about life in the Bronx in that era. (Since my grandparents stayed on Sedgwick Avenue when we moved to Connecticut, I continued to visit regularly through the 1960s.) After my ejaculation of enthusiasm, De Niro politely agreed that the film's writer had captured the time perfectly. The star himself had not been to Sedgwick Avenue, since for budgetary reasons they had recreated our neighbourhood in Queens.

Have you ever thought about how our year together seems in retrospect Year One in American popular culture? 'Rock Around the Clock' by Bill Haley and his Comets began the rock era, and Elvis Presley had his first number one on any chart ('I Forgot to Remember to Forget' topped the country and western list). Disneyland opened while Disney TV shows *Adventures of Davy Crockett* and *The Mickey Mouse Club* inspired crazes for wearing coonskin caps and mouse ears, though not at the same time. The movie stars the world still prefers to remember as the symbols of America were at their peak in 1955: James Dean became immortal in *Rebel Without a Cause* and eternal in a car crash; Marilyn Monroe unsuccessfully held down her billowing skirt in *The Seven Year Itch*; Marlon Brando won an Oscar for his previous year's work in *On the Waterfront*. It was a special year, Henry, a year which gave us the heroes that have lasted our country a lifetime. If you are not a psychiatrist, perhaps you are a sociologist now and can explain to me how they have endured. In the meantime I will wonder if we would have remained pals had we stayed in the same school. Would we have been famous friends? Could we have been contenders?

Henry, I know everyone's childhood seems innocent compared to their adult years, and there are probably even some children in Bosnia and Northern Ireland who will grow up thinking that the 1990s were a special time. But the Bronx we knew was preferable to the Bronx we have now, isn't it? I don't have a single memory of menace. I don't even recall being chaperoned to the park or the soda shop by adults. My mother assures me there always was one, but the noteworthy thing is that I don't remember them being there. We didn't notice them because we didn't feel we needed them to protect us. We weren't afraid of being caught in the crossfire of somebody else's gunfight, as New York ghetto kids are today. And, of course, our street wasn't in a ghetto then. I don't know what you would call it now, but I do know that, when I last went back to the old neighbourhood, part of it wasn't. Literally. It was gone, empty spaces left where buildings had been felled or torched. Does your childhood home still stand?

We were too young in 1954–5 to have learned anything about sex except, perhaps, that the stork lived in the same mythical land as Santa Claus. But have you seen the recent histories of homosexual New York which point out that the years between the Depression and the Stonewall riot in 1969, which began the modern gay rights movement, were the low point of the century for gays in the city? It seems that Mayor Fiorello LaGuardia, who I had thought as a child was such a nice man for having read the comics over the radio during a newspaper strike, had authorized police enticement and entrapment of homosexuals, and literally tens of thousands of men had been convicted during the thirty or so years before Mayor Lindsay – a Republican, not a Democrat! – called off the sordid practice. It is disgusting that 'pretty policemen' seduced gay men, acting as the twentieth-century equivalents of the Sirens in *The Odyssey* who lured Greek sailors to their deaths, with the toilets of New York City replacing the rocks of the seashore. If that doesn't make the practice sound preposterous, consider that my great grandfather was a New York policeman in the 1890s. I would have considered it beneath his dignity to have dressed rough or in frills to entice civilians into a victimless embrace. The families of the policemen who enticed gays into propositioning them ought to have been horrified that this was how they were earning their living, and so should the law officers themselves. This is all the more reason to extol Mayor Lindsay and forgive him for not having the snow in Queens ploughed promptly (a lapse which legend says cost him the next election). I am even more proud that at the London première of the 1980s revival of *Anything Goes* I inexplicably encountered him in an aisle during intermission, and he introduced himself to me! I felt complimented for about two seconds and then realized that, even twenty years later, the campaigning habits of a politician die hard.

I must pause to modify something I just said about not remembering adults walking with us around the neighbourhood. I do remember being accompanied by my grandmother to the soda shop on two occasions. The first time I had a milk shake and then, for some obscure medical reason, promptly vomited. I remember the concern of the storekeeper, who inquired about my health and wasn't angry at five-year-old me for chucking up all over his floor only feet from where other patrons were still eating. (Would he yell at me today or shoot me?) And I recall the attention of my grandmother, who was solely concerned with my well-being and didn't even entertain the notion of being embarrassed by my barfing behaviour. This woman loved us, let there be no doubt. On another occasion, when I only needed one player to complete the second set of the year's baseball cards, she took me to the soda shop and bought me a whole box of Topps bubble gum and cards. You never saw more bubble gum thrown out in one day in your whole life. Today I can't remember whether I got the card or not – I don't even remember the name of the player. But I treasure the memory of my grandmother caring enough to do something to which she was completely indifferent because she knew it was important to me.

Our neighbours liked her too. Did you know that, shortly after we were in kindergarten, our teacher had a son who she named Paul? And did you know that, as he grew up, he announced that my grandmother was his best friend? Were you aware he called her 'Maudie darling', visited her often and did favours for her in her old age? And did you know, Henry, that after my grandmother had lived a full life and died in her mid-eighties, this Paul sent me a long letter expressing his grief and affection? And did you know that this Paul did not get to live a full life, that he became infected with HIV and died of AIDS while he was still a young man?

Is it possible that, in the chronology of our lifetimes, futures which were once not even conceivable can link us to our pasts? Here I am, Henry, writing to a man who will almost certainly never see this and quite possibly does not even exist, talking to you across the miles and across the years, speaking to you as a modern-day patron of Britain's leading AIDS charity about a boy from our block who died too young to benefit from leading AIDS charities; who died too young period.

Of the two Pauls, Henry, I was the lucky one. I got out

of the Bronx, avoided AIDS and lived beyond my youth. Did you? I hope so. Whoever you are, wherever you are, I have always loved you.

SCOTT

I owe my career to sex. That sounds more exciting than
it is. I owe my career to sex I wouldn't have, rather
than something I did. I also owe my career to you. As Chief
Announcer you placed me in the news training course at the
Dartmouth College radio station, WDCR, and you gave me a
regular disc jockey show when, for reasons of chastity, I was
bounced out of the news department.

Dartmouth in the late 1960s was still all male. No one
considered it might be a breeding ground for gays and,
indeed, the environment seemed vigorously monosexual
rather than homosexual. I participated in all the great
he-man rituals, including riding on a flatbed truck into the
New Hampshire mountains to gather railroad ties from a
derelict line for a class of '70 bonfire.

The experience was incredibly cold, dangerous and
astonishingly exciting. When we got back to town, we piled
the railroad ties into seventy tiers, slinking up and down the
structure like spidermen. We were filled with such pride we
felt we were participating in the most important task on the
planet, let alone the campus. I ran to WDCR to broadcast an
appeal for more freshman volunteers. It didn't occur to me
that I was barging in on a classical music programme and
that the disc jockey was loathe to lower the tone of his classy
show. My enthusiasm melted his reserve and in between
the Beethoven and the Brahms came the bonfire.

I naively thought that all Dartmouth men loved to carry
railroad ties and climb seventy tiers of rotting wood. I soon
learned they were a minority, but I still had no idea that
some of those who did could be gay. I had not learned of
the diversity of the homosexual population, and so was
completely unprepared for my first Dartmouth seduction
scene.

I was not merely ignorant about gay life. I was in the dark about sex, period.

Religious inhibitions helped keep me from any early experimentation. My father's parents had been Italian immigrants, both Catholics, and my mother's father was also of the Roman Church. My maternal grandmother assumed a vague Protestantism, which my brothers and I considered mildly eccentric, but in hindsight appears heroic in view of the number of Catholics around her. Catholic statues were placed in some rooms of our house and holy water at the bottom of a staircase.

As a youngster I was deeply religious. I took seriously the warnings of nuns in Sunday School who told us a young person they knew had died suddenly while asleep and it could happen to any of us. I feared hellfire and considered the sisters' suggestion that I become a priest. When I first heard a fellow pupil swear on a school bus, I came home crying. I had to be pure, to avoid what one Catholic prayer called 'the near occasions of sin', so I could escape damnation or a hopelessly long time in limbo. To the latter end I noted the number of days, months and years of remission from limbo offered by each prayer in my missal, and made sure I frequently recited those which gave most days off per word. The retention skills I later showed for aspects of popular music were applied by my seven-year-old self to the Catholic catechism. I memorized the commandments and admonitions of the Church, portions of the Mass and lists of venial and mortal sins.

The first dent in my confidence in the clergy came when I was ten. A friend came over to me in class and showed me a page from a book of geometrical designs. I could not avert my eyes quickly enough. The mathematical figures resembled human buttocks.

I yearned for the opportunity to go to confession to be pardoned for this terrible sin. I had witnessed a vile vulgarity. Alas, it was Monday and confessions were heard on Saturday afternoons. I spent the week dreading the moment I would have to tell the priest of my wickedness.

When the time came, I snuck into the confessional and began the sacrament. 'Bless me, father, I confess to almighty God and to you, father, that I have sinned. My last confession was two weeks ago. These are my sins.'

I proceeded to throw in a few venial offences. I wanted to get the priest bored so he wouldn't notice the big one floating by.

'Answering back to my parents twice . . . arguing with my brothers . . . fighting . . . looking at . . . '

I had so feared this moment I hadn't considered how I would phrase it. Looking at a book of mathematical designs, one of which resembled someone's backside? Looking at circles drawn with a compass?

'Looking at – pictures.'

'My son,' the priest intervened, sensing my distress, 'we all get the temptation to look at lewd pictures of women.' What? Who said anything about women? 'But there will come a time when you will meet a girl who is right for you and you will settle down together . . . ' No! No! I was more sinful than I thought. I was making a priest wrong! 'For your penance say five Our Fathers and ten Hail Marys . . . '

While reciting the paean to the Virgin, I surmised that the reason the priest had misinterpreted my sin was because he couldn't read my mind. If he didn't know what I was thinking, he couldn't be the direct representative on earth of an all-knowing God.

This was my first doubt about the Catholic Church. My confidence and interest in the faith gradually ebbed away. During my first term at Dartmouth and away from home I stopped going to church every Sunday. The college's Catholic chaplain, Father Bill Nolan, expressed dismay, saying this was the first step down a road which ended with doubts about the very divinity of Christ. I assured him I would not go that far, but stopped going to church nonetheless.

The complete break occurred unpredictably. It was dinner time in Thayer Hall one Friday. I didn't like the fish dish on offer and wanted the meat. I knew well the prohibition against eating meat on Fridays. To do so was to purchase a one-way ticket to hell.

I bought the meat meal. For moments I stared at it, wondering if I dare take a bite. I took a nibble tentatively. It tasted as good as it did the other six days of the week, so I took another. I waited for lightning to strike me down, but none was forthcoming.

I finished the meal and walked back to my room very carefully, hoping to avoid a catastrophic accident. When, after a couple of hours, nothing detrimental to my health had occurred, I ceased worrying. I had seen through the sham of the Catholic Church and lived. I went through a period of anger at the restrictions the faith had led me to impose on my life and then gradually became more flippant about it.

My Catholicism didn't stop me from having normal childish emotions. In second grade I had a crush on Mary Bess Walker. I had a competitor, a classmate named George. We seven-year-olds would vie for Mary Bess's attention during recess. Greens Farms School, Westport was over-crowded, so the second grade had been farmed out to a nearby church with a large lawn, or at least what was a lawn until we kids got through trampling all over it every weekday for nine months. Our year at the church ended with George and I having wooed to a draw.

For third grade we moved back to Greens Farms School itself, an imposing two-level brick building built on a hill with a single-storey extension not too convincingly matched to the original style. This year was one of the most crucial in my education. My teacher was Miss Ruth Charlton, one of those inspiring school teachers every President of the United States claims to have had, but few of the rest of us are ever fortunate enough to run into. Miss Charlton (even now it would seem disrespectful to call her

Ruth) was both a strict taskmaster and a great humanist. Perhaps because she was unmarried, she shared with us some of the things she enjoyed like E. B. White's wonderful children's book *Charlotte's Web*.

It was in Miss Charlton's class that I met the best friend of my childhood, Eric Tomassi. Several things bound me to Eric, the most obvious being that we both had Italian names. We also each had brothers a year younger than ourselves, which made for a natural foursome on trips to the movies and bowling alley.

Eric was intellectually brilliant. Since it was not fair on Eric to be isolated in class simply because he was the best reader, Miss Charlton gave him me. In the last third of the school year we were moved into fourth grade math and social studies classes, and that September we 'skipped' fourth and went to the fifth grade together.

Eric and I inevitably became competitors in certain ways. When I became infatuated with Betsy Paget, I encouraged the rumour that Eric was besotted with Christine Cook and actually linked them romantically in a ludicrous humorous poem I delivered to the class. One day I took this precocious sexuality too far: I kissed Betsy on the cheek in the hallway outside Miss Charlton's room.

It was a brazen act, comparable to streaking in adulthood. There was no way it could go unnoticed. Our teacher told me I shouldn't have done it and must not do it again. I was mortified. I had been caught kissing a girl at the age of eight. I vowed then and there to retire from such acts, at least in public, and for many years I feared that my friend Jack, Betsy's athletic brother, would get nasty on me. I need not have worried. Besides being well built, Jack was an altar boy at St Luke's Church and would never have resorted to fisticuffs.

After Eric and I had 'skipped' fourth grade together we became closer than ever, partly because of the mere fact that we knew nobody else in our new surroundings. Our greatest triumph came when we were inducted into Denis

O'Neill's secret fraternity, where we were each given nicknames. Denis called himself 'Frenchie', a rather cosmopolitan choice for such a young lad, and Eric got labelled 'Motts' in honour of a popular brand of apple sauce. O'Neill christened me 'Gambo', the first person to call me by that moniker. Wherever I have gone in life people have started calling me Gambo. When I first got involved in the London music business and Linda McCartney unexpectedly called me Gambo, I just thought, can't stop it, might as well enjoy it. I doubt, however, that Meryl Streep ever referred to Denis as 'Frenchie' when she filmed his script *The River Wild*.

I was delighted to receive any sign of acceptance from our new fifth-grade classmates, so an invitation to Lynne Betts's party was a summons. Lynne was a tall girl for a fifth-grader, and my feelings towards her were ones of appreciation rather than attachment. The night of her party I got a chance to show my feelings for another Greens Farms girl in a direct way.

The party was held in the basement, a site more practical than romantic. Children could have their own self-contained world down there without interference from parents. That Lynne did not expect her elders to interrupt became obvious when she acquiesced to a game of Spin the Bottle.

I don't recall who suggested this childish contest, in which guests sat on the floor in a circle. The person who spun the bottle had to kiss the member of the opposite sex it pointed to when it came to rest. If the bottle pointed at someone of the same sex, it got a quick re-spin.

There was certainly a great number of closet Casanovas in class because at the mere mention of the game many of my mates started leering with lust. Mindful of my illicit Paget peck of the previous year, I was at first terrified at the prospect of having to kiss someone in public, but I soon warmed to the game.

Some of my friends grew bored with Spin the Bottle and decided to take things further. Trey and Joyce briefly retired to a closet, too briefly to do anything with lasting consequences, but long enough to share something more than a kiss. Of course they may have been doing nothing more than examining the Betts family linen, but my imagination, kindled by Spin the Bottle, was now aflame. It appeared to me that this innocent gathering had degenerated into a make-out party with couples pairing off for seconds-long intervals.

It is an American cultural legend that at such affairs in the late 1950s and early 1960s the obligatory make-out music was 'Johnny's Greatest Hits' by Johnny Mathis. I can confirm that it was indeed Mathis who cooed 'It's Not for Me to Say' and 'Wonderful! Wonderful!' as Trey and Joyce hid in the closet, and other couples retired to the couch.

Ma and Pa Betts may not have worried too much about what their charges were up to, but they certainly were upset when the basement lights flashed on and off for five minutes. Was there an electrical fault? Was a child injured? Mr Betts stuck his head around the door and urgently enquired, 'What's going on here?'

He was reassured that we energetic kids were just fooling around, but ruled we could only continue the party if we left the lights on. This put a bit of a dampener on the proceedings because, no matter how precociously passionate we were, we didn't want to let anybody see us at it.

Except me. I felt slightly left out of things, rather ashamed that I hadn't been flailing my limbs around with the rest of the guests. I decided that, in the interests of being liked and respected by my new classmates, I should demonstrate my boyhood before I went home. There was no one in my eyes more suitable for demonstrating boyhood with than Cynthia Carey, a winsome girl with the promise of a fine figure and a face like an angel. No matter what she might do, no girl who looked that pure could ever be debased.

Again, except by me. In a moment of theatrical bravado I put my right arm around her waist and leaned over her until the top half of her body was almost parallel to the ground. I started caressing her feverishly like Rudolph Valentino on speed. This posture invited collapse, so I carried her over to the couch and lay on top of her, continuing my uninterrupted kissing.

I thought I was merely mimicking a Hollywood romance. From her lack of resistance I suspect Cynthia realized this. When I looked to the right over my pretend paramour's head to see who had arrived at the basement door, however, I saw to my horror her older brother, come to drive her home. It was apparent he had not entered the basement of the Betts' house expecting to find his twelve-year-old sister lying on a settee with an eleven-year-old boy on top of her making fully clothed love like a rapist in training.

Cynthia got up and joined her brother. We did not share a goodnight kiss. We never kissed again. She soon left the Westport school system. Six years later, when she entered Westfair Pharmacy, where I was working part-time during the summer, she showed no sign of recognition. It was just as well. I wouldn't have wanted her to think of me as part of the hired help.

I was mortified by the Betts party and vowed to live it down. For several years I neither touched nor pursued pubescent girls. I thought I had lost my lustful image until one afternoon, three years after the fateful party, Denis O'Neill's mother gave me a lift home from school.

'By the way, Paul,' she remarked as she neared our driveway, 'I hear you're really a ladies' man. Denis told me about the party at Lynne Betts's . . . '

I could have shrivelled into a raisin. It seemed the Statute of Limitations on that party would never run out. Though I resumed kissing girls in high school, I did nothing that might embarrass me and, if ever I was asked what kind of girl I would marry, I religiously replied it would be a good Catholic girl.

There was another reason why I avoided girls for a few years. Linda Easton had turned me off. This may come as a surprise, particularly to Linda Easton, but my first sight of a naked female body was not only shocking but also disgusting. The Eastons lived across the street from us at the end of a long drive. Their backyard was a veritable woodland, with a tiny spot of water with land in it that served as my personal Treasure Island. This forest was dark and deep, as nature had intended Westport to be before the developers came to town, and my brother Peter and I frequently forayed into it with his classmate Dale and a neighbour of the same age, Paul.

One day Dale's younger sister Linda gestured to us to come into the woods. She had something to show us. I think it was because we always left her out of our games that she felt she had to bid for attention, but armchair psychology thirty-odd years later doesn't convey the impact of what she did next. Linda dropped her trousers and stood before us amongst the trees stark naked, cackling like some Wicked Witch of the West.

Sex education wasn't so good in Westport schools. As a matter of fact, it didn't exist. Even when you got to a compulsory course called 'Health' in junior high, it consisted mostly of tips like washing under your arms to prevent body odour. Never having had a sister and never having been a peeper, it had never occurred to me that girls didn't have all the same appendages boys did.

'Castration anxiety' was hardly the description of my reaction. Try 'panic'. Fixed to the spot for what seemed like an eternity, I finally got sufficient adrenalin flowing to flee. But this forest was no flat stretch. I ran about five yards and tripped over a large half-buried root, falling head first to the earth. I had the presence of mind to put my hands out to break my fall. I did not have the vision to see that I was putting my hands squarely into a pile of fresh dog faeces and pushing into it with all my body weight.

The end of the world could not be more horrific than this half minute of my childhood. I sped home to wash off this foul-smelling smudge. My mother helped me clean my hands, performing a disgusting chore that only maternal love could bring a person to do.

Freudians in the audience may frolic, speculating on how for the rest of my life I have associated the vagina with dogshit. I did not seek nor look at another female's nude frame for years. Consequently I was in for another shock when the summer before I went to Dartmouth I met Judy and John at Compo Beach. Judy was wearing a bathing suit so tight in the crotch that her pubic hairs spilled out on either side. Neither Judy nor John seemed aware of this indiscretion and smiled and chatted amiably while I blithered outwardly and went into deep shock inwardly. They say the Lord giveth and the Lord taketh away. He had taken away Linda Easton's penis, now he had given Judy pubic hair. This new jolt put me off women for a good few more months.

My Catholicism discouraged contact with girls and so did the undue affection clause of our high school offences code. 'Undue affection' was an offence punished by detention after school. One spinster Latin teacher seemed to delight in busting young teens for this, and I always dreaded it when an amorous girl sat in my lap, fearing that this diminutive enforcer would leap from behind a bush and yell, 'Hehhehhehhehhehhehhehheh, undue affection!'

I personally far preferred putting an affectionate arm around a friend's shoulders to considering serious sex play. When the first opportunity to have sex with a male friend came, I was genuinely shocked. It occurred in the period between the commencement of departing seniors and the beginning of the summer term, a fortnight in June traditionally reserved at Dartmouth for alumni reunions. Some students lingered on campus after the end of the academic year for 'dorm clerking', serving as receptionist-cum-concierges at dormitories housing returning graduates. This was an easy source of good money, particularly as the gratuities were generous.

The college made interim room arrangements for dorm clerks. It didn't really matter where or with whom you were because you were hardly ever there. The period was so short you wouldn't make new friends anyway.

I happened to be put in a room with one of the newsmen from the radio station and a taciturn third whose name never really registered. One morning the newsman and I returned from WDCR having done *Daybreak* together, and napped before our next assignment. Doing the disc jockey side of the show was new to me and I was still in my mind fundamentally a newsman. I was just beginning to relish the opportunity for expression and the feeling of power that came with this kind of work.

My alarm went off at around 10.30, indicating that I had about half an hour before I had to prepare the noon news. I was about to slip back into my reporter's clothes like the quick-change artist we summer staffers had all become. Suddenly, from the bunk below, I heard the voice of my friend Carl. (This wasn't his real name and there wasn't anybody called Carl in the news department at the time. He may have changed my life then, but I am in no mind to change his now.)

'Do you think our room-mate gives blow jobs?' he asked.

'I don't know, why don't you ask him?' I replied, treating the enquiry as facetiously as I thought it was intended.

'Will you blow me?' Carl rejoined.

This was not the answer I had expected. I was, at the age of eighteen, still unaware of the tenderness that can exist between men. Carl had with four simple words introduced me to a world where men who loved each other did something more than thinking nice thoughts. I was terrified. I first asked him if he was really serious. When he assured me he was, I refused his request. He then offered to service me. I coined an instant statement of policy: 'I will neither blow nor be blown.'

For forty-five minutes Carl tried to convert me, while I

determinedly stayed in my bed, ludicrously believing that if I lay face down I was protecting myself from sexual assault.

'Don't you wish you had a human body up there next to you?'

'No,' I replied.

'Haven't you ever had one next to you?'

'No,' I replied.

'Haven't you ever masturbated?'

'No,' I replied.

'You haven't?' His enquiry turned to incredulity.

'No . . .'

'That's weird.'

The last thing I wanted to do was come out of this encounter thinking I was strange, but I had no time to ponder the matter, for Carl's questions kept flying like an all-out sexual first strike.

'Did you know you have a feminine ass?' he asked.

I didn't have a ready retort. I hadn't contemplated my backside, and there was the terrible prospect he might be right.

Fortunately I had a polite out: I had to do 'the twelve'. But this escape didn't end my new suitor's overtures. Crossing the green later that day our paths happened to intersect and, as he passed, Carl muttered into my ear, 'I still want to be blown.'

This time I felt more annoyed than threatened. I sought solace from you, Scott. You were my mentor.

The day Carl propositioned me it was natural I should pour out the whole lurid tale to you. To my slight disappointment your initial reaction was not, 'I'll take care of you,' but rather, 'Pervert! What a pervert!' You finally did promise to protect me if things somehow came to the crunch and, armed with that assurance, I felt I could face Carl in any alleyway.

I now confess for the first time that, in giving you an impression of my pursuer's plans, I gave Carl a worse reputation than he deserved. One evening, while you were out of the dorm room we shared that summer in Ripley Hall, I grew particularly troubled over one of Carl's remarks. 'That's weird,' he had said when I revealed I had never masturbated. I never wanted to give anybody a chance to say that about me, so I decided to masturbate on the spot.

Unfortunately I had no idea how to do it. For the past couple of years I had found regular relief in wet dreams, but the images of which they consisted were hardly enough to stimulate an erection when conscious. I wasn't even aware one was supposed to fantasize. I just stood in the bathroom and knocked myself about for a minute or two until I thought the procedure so ridiculous I lay down on the living-room couch for a nap.

This was a big mistake. When I awoke about fifteen minutes later, I discovered to my horror that, while asleep, I had ejaculated all over the sofa. (I never again napped without my trousers on.) I was panicked that you would return to the room, find evidence of my wayward sexuality and throw what we used to call a 'shit fit', a temper tantrum.

I cleaned the settee as best I could and went to bed, hoping against hope that you would, upon your return, go straight to the bedroom without turning the light on in the living-room. I hoped in vain. Immediately after you opened the door you turned on the light. Within seconds I heard a shriek of disgust.

'Yuccccccccccck!' you screamed. 'Carl's been here!'

Carl? What did he have to do with it?

'He's come in here and beat off over the couch thinking about you! Disgusting!'

Disgusting? Delightful! You had proved a true friend in the most difficult circumstances by providing me with an alibi I hadn't even considered. Relieved to be blameless in the 204 Ripley Sex Stain Affair, I have never corrected you – until now. This was one visit to our room Carl never made.

He did make others, though, asking me to massage his chest or inveighing against me because I hadn't gone to a party he was at, but had instead gone to see your rock group, The Ham Sandwich. I never knew that summer when the next outburst or advance would be nor what form it would take. It could verge on emotional blackmail, as when he solemnly intoned, 'I stared at razor blades this afternoon thinking of you,' or it could be laughingly melodramatic, as in the Great Shower Showdown.

As Local News Director it was my responsibility to be first in the Tri-Town with the big area stories. One day the UPI wire announced the appointment of Hanover's first Town Manager, Neil Berlin. Carl confronted me with this fact as I dried myself in the Ripley shower room.

'You missed the Town Manager story!' he screamed.

'I did not!' I insisted. 'The Selectmen promised they'd give me the story first. It's not my fault if they went back on their word.'

'Yes it is!' he howled. 'You're supposed to get the story first and it doesn't matter how you get it, whether the Selectmen keep their word or not.'

I was provoked beyond the threshold of my tolerance. In those days I only got mad in public about once a year, but, when I did, mine was the wrath of the Furies. This was my outburst for 1967.

'Shut up!' the normally sweet me bellowed. 'I've had enough from you! I'm working just as hard as you this summer, maybe harder! I get up first to turn on the station, I do *Daybreak*, I go to my courses, I do the noon, I do *Sounds*, I do my half of the six, what else do you want? I can't do any more. I might feel guilty if I was to blame, but I'm not. I'm doing my job, so just shut up and leave me alone!'

I had never yelled at anyone that way, and I feared the reprisal which seemed inevitable, but never came.

'You know what?' Carl said softly, in complete contrast to my high decibel count. 'You're beautiful when you're mad.'

38

What sounded like a bad Hollywood script had been played out in real life. I could not handle the pressure of not knowing when I would next be propositioned, of feeling I was somehow responsible for whether Carl slit his wrists or not. I resigned my position as Local News Director to get away from him.

You asked for the reason behind my decision and I told you. Perhaps in sympathy, perhaps in belief, you gave me a regular disc jockey assignment that autumn, and in time I became the Tri-Town area's top-rated deejay. It was completely unintended, but I had been steered out of news into jocking by the sex I wouldn't have – and by you, the best upperclassman friend a naive college student ever had. It could well be that every music radio programme I have ever presented has been made possible, in part, by you. Thank you, Scott. You gave me a good life.

DAVID

I don't want to do this. I really don't want to do this. You want to know how badly I don't want to do this? I finished the second letter of this book six weeks ago. I knew I wanted to write this one next. I had ten days to go before I went on vacation to New York, so I didn't start this straightaway. I rationalized that it would be horrible if I found myself in mid-flow when it was time to go to the States, because I would spend the entire holiday with the rest of this letter floating around in my head, demanding to be written. I disciplined myself to have an actual break while I was in America, so I didn't start this during those twelve days. I arrived back and spent a couple of days sorting out the mail and the messages that had accumulated in my absence. Then, with my personal assistant away for a week, I comforted myself that it was more important to clear up the backlog of pressing correspondence than to begin this letter. Then I got a cold and managed to avoid anything too physically or mentally strenuous for a week in the interests of my health.

This hasn't been just a writer's block, David, this has been a writer's Iron Curtain. But even though I am still sniffling, I am finally typing. I now know why I didn't want to start this letter. I have written you many letters in the past, but this one will be the last. I don't know how I will feel when I have said everything there is to say. When there are no words left, I don't know what feelings will remain.

For years, when people have asked me what my favourite movies are, we deal with *Citizen Kane* for a few minutes and then I mention *Mean Streets*. Besides its many objective virtues, I tell them that it has a special significance for me. I say, but for a couple of spins of the wheel of fate, I could have been the Harvey Keitel character. Sure, I wasn't brought up in Little Italy, but I was born in the Bronx, the grandson of Italian immigrants on my father's side, and had two or three things not happened, like moving to Connecticut when I was nearly six, I could have been drawn into the ethnic world of those Scorsese creations. I have certainly known a Johnny Boy or two in my time.

But, as the prospect of writing you this letter has caused me to reflect, I realize there was more of a chance that I might have turned out to be very much like you, and vice versa. We both were raised Catholic boys in Fairfield County, went to Dartmouth College in New Hampshire and progressed to the big cities – you to New York and I to London via Oxford to follow our dreams in show business. We both suffered to come to terms with a sexuality that was first impossible, then inadvisable and finally a blessing.

We often spoke of how non-prepared we were to deal with our sexuality. Not just ill-prepared, non-prepared. We could not say that homosexuality was condemned in our churches or our schools during the early 1960s because it wasn't mentioned. It didn't exist. We were not taught that it was a possibility. I suppose news must have filtered down to us that somewhere on some strange planet there were men who preferred each other's company – I recall a front page *New York Times* piece telling of a witch hunt for homosexuals in the federal government that was referred to as a 'vice' purge. But the Catholic Church and the school system failed us totally as regards letting us know who we might be and in whose illustrious company we might find ourselves. Negroes, Jews and other groups nobly fought discrimination during our adolescence, but at least they knew not only who they were but also that they were. We were denied these fundamental facts, you in Greenwich, I in Westport. The homo-erotic feelings we had in high school must have been 'just a phase', because there was no flower into which they could blossom.

43

I found the first mention of homosexuality in high school coming from my own mouth. We were studying Greek literature in English class during my senior year. Some guys and gals, those ancient Greeks, providing the first socially approved role models for half the young bent population of the Western world. They even lent us the name of one of their islands, Lesbos. Unlike condescending pedants who complain that the perfectly wonderful English word 'gay' was ruined by its application to male homosexuals, Lesbians do not appear to have ever complained about 'lesbians'.

So there we were in English class, studying Greek playwrights and philosophers known only by single names like Aristophanes, Euripides and Socrates, the forerunners of Cher, Seal and Sting. The teacher said we would notice that it was socially acceptable in Athens to love members of one's own sex, particularly across generations.

'Hey, don't knock homosexuals,' I blurted out. 'I love homosexuals.'

It was a gag line and it had the class in stiches. I was president of the student government and a bit of a wit, so I got away with it without any of my schoolmates questioning me, although I do recall the teacher turning red and going 'hehhehheh' under his breath. Looking back years later, I was amazed I could so freely and openly make a statement that seemed a joke, but was literally true, something which would have been proscribed in almost any other circumstance, but was actually approved in the particular. It was also the first time I could make that declaration about myself and the last for some years to come. It was not possible homosexual teenagers could exist. It was as if we aspired to be a Purple People Eater. Everyone had heard of one, but nobody thought such a thing really existed. Nine years later, when I informed my best friend from high school of my sexuality, he told me to stop being ridiculous: 'You're the least homosexual person I know.'

The silence continued at Dartmouth. Maybe the two

years that separated us, I being class of 1970 and you '72, made a difference, but from your reports I don't think so. You told me how astonished you were by your first sexual encounter, and I was certainly as nonplussed when I was propositioned for the first time. It seems ridiculous that on what was then an all-male campus no one ever mentioned homosexuality, but it was partly because it was an all-male campus that nobody ever mentioned it. The whole concept – keeping 3,000 young men at the peak of their sexual powers dozens of miles from women, while assuming that they would never be tempted to turn to each other for relief – was so preposterous it would collapse under the weight of its own ludicrousness if it were ever questioned.

My very first television appearance was on the New Hampshire public television station, Channel 31. The channel was doing a documentary on what was then the red-hot issue of co-education, and I was chosen as one of a couple of model students to give my opinion on the virtues of admitting women to the college. I calmly explained that I was in favour of co-education because it was natural for men and women to mix. I cited my room-mate Pete, an outstanding man and a drop-dead handsome guy, who worried sometimes if he was inadequate simply because he didn't have a woman in his life. I found it outrageously unfair that fine young men like Pete should doubt themselves simply because they were deprived every day of female companionship by their elders.

I thought these remarks were completely reasonable, but you should have seen the Director of the College News Service wince and throw back his head in anguish while I made them. The admission of women was a hot issue at Dartmouth in 1970, and I could just see the Director counting the lost donations from alumni outraged by young Gambaccini questioning the sanctity of their treasured all-male idyll of memory.

I wasn't questioning the marvel of their experiences, of course; I was bemoaning the predicament of our generation. Denied the opportunity to be practising hetero-sexuals, except on orgiastic weekends, Dartmouth students were certainly not going to discuss the option of being practising homosexuals, and the subject was closed before it was opened.

I found I was approached by other men more off campus than on, and this was inevitably sordid and comic rather than sublime and beautiful. On one occasion I was at the Doral Hotel in Miami Beach on a long weekend, having persuaded my generous father that I needed a break after my hard work during the 1968 autumn term. One night I went to see Tiny Tim of 'Tip-Toe Thru' the Tulips with Me' fame in another of the leading hotels on the beachfront. As I walked back to the Doral, I was stopped by a motorist who asked me if I wanted a lift. This was the reverse of hitch-hiking, and I was so taken by the novelty and generosity of it all that I didn't suspect the man might have ulterior motives.

About a quarter of a mile down the road my well-groomed and polite new friend started telling me about what he had been doing on his holidays.

'My friend Joe and I got talking to these two girls,' he recalled, 'one blonde, one brunette, both with big tits.' He looked over to me to see if I was still paying attention, which I was, politely, although I did wish he'd keep his eyes on the road.

'We managed to get them back to the hotel, and we each took a bed. I started with the blonde, he had the brunette.' Again he looked over to see if I was listening, but he had hardly said anything to make me jump out of the car.

'We were really doing it. Fucking, sucking, everything.'

And I played a round of golf today, I thought.

'When we'd done everything, we changed girls. I tell you, it was something.' Another sideways glance. He doesn't even know me and he's telling me all this personal stuff . . .

'And when that was over, we were bored. So we started in on each other.'

Oh, I get it. There's a punch line to this. And it's going to be . . .

'Gives you half a hard-on just thinking about it, doesn't it?'

No, it doesn't, I thought, but that's not what I told him. What I said was . . .

'I think I better get out here.'

To his credit, without a word, my oversexed pal, who had just become frightfully undersexed, pulled over to the side of the road, silently accepted my thanks for the ride and drove off. Whether he invited anyone else into his car that night and whether that person got half or even three-quarters of a hard-on I have never wondered until now.

For I had another suitor to contend with the next day. Just before lunch I went to the sauna in the Doral. In 1969, this was still an exotic facility for a hotel. As I walked from the showers, a tall balding man of about fifty stopped me and looked down at my appendage.

'Is that all yours?' he shrieked. 'You stay here and I'll be right back!'

I don't know if he came right back, because I didn't stay to find out. I set a personal best for the sauna-to-hotel-room dash.

Nothing had prepared me for these propositions. Two years of Dartmouth had cocooned me from the universe of sexual possibilities. It seemed the minute I left the Hanover plain I was destined to be shocked by the realities of relationships in the Wide, Wide World. This wasn't just true of young gays and bisexuals: Dartmouth alumni had, in the late 1970s, the highest divorce rate of any American university's graduates. It seemed that the way we were forced to learn to live without women on campus helped make it impossible for us to live with them later.

The worst by-product of the isolation was the inevitable casting of females as lust objects. Not sex objects, lust objects. Because Dartmouth men did not have young women in their everyday lives, they were desperate to have sex with the ones they finally did see on weekends. My friends and I used to marvel at the way buses of students from what were called 'girls' schools' arrived on Friday afternoons and evenings. These were like coaches of cows at the conclusion of a weekly cattle drive, ready for branding by the hot pokers of the Big Green ranchers.

I'm not naive enough to think the women didn't compare their opinions of their hosts, but I have to wonder if even girl-talk matched the tone of the men in my dorm.

'You should have seen her!' Bob enthused about his last date. 'A twelve-inch pubic spread!'

'She fucks like a bunny!' marvelled Barry, who obviously had enjoyed at least one previous weekend with a rabbit. 'We kept at it all night, she kept wanting it. A personal record, eight times in one night!'

I recall asking Barry at what number he would begin facing a danger of death.

'I don't believe I got stuck with her,' Rob said of his blind date. 'She wore a tie!'

'The worst,' sympathized Mike. 'She makes her own clothes!'

This became a catchphrase around the dorm. 'She makes her own clothes!' was the taunt to tease anyone who had an arranged encounter with someone he'd never seen.

Sometimes the cowpunchers went out to round up the herd. 'Road trips' were necessary because the nearest universities for female students were over a hundred miles away, a junior college being a mere fifty miles down the road for those whose intellectual demands were tempered by sexual needs. Anyone with a car became a celebrity among his dorm-mates or fraternity brothers.

And I had a car, courtesy of my folks, who would be relieved to know that I only ever escorted friends on road trips three times. On one occasion I managed to cross the Vermont/New York state line with thirteen people in my Plymouth Sport Fury. This was an incredible achievement, and not just for the number of people in the vehicle.

Because police patrolled the border looking for student drivers capitalizing on New York's lower drinking age, we had to appear as if the thirteen persons were only six. This was achieved by having six people sitting, five people on the floor at their feet, and the two who drew the short straws packed into the trunk. Every time I see *White Heat* or *Goodfellas* I cringe at the sequences of people in the boot, knowing I transported two Dartmouth students across state lines, assuming, without knowing for sure, that their oxygen would hold out.

At the time of this particular trip I was under intense pressure to leave the GAU. This was my fraternity's acronym for Grand Army of the Unlaid. Our big brothers felt it was their responsibility to motivate us to lose our virginity. Incredibly enough, all we pledges honestly revealed our membership or departure from the GAU. At one point the Army had been reduced to a foot patrol of just a Southern boy named Ricky and myself. Ricky's will was whetted by drink, which also negatively affected his pulling and his performance, so he had to wait for the night when he attracted a girl through the window of opportunity while he was simultaneously horny and sober. This night finally came. The fraternity immediately threw a party for Ricky, during which he passed out from drink.

I was the only private left in the Grand Army of the Unlaid. I didn't want to have sex with anyone just to please my brothers. For this and other reasons, I left the house.

This was in the spring of 1968, a few months before you arrived on campus. We were not as close at Dartmouth as we would become a few years later in New York City. Because I was the class of 1970 and you were '72, we only became friends towards the end of my four years in Hanover. I best remember moments with you on the Glee Club tour in the spring of 1970. You were a talented singer; I was one of the three narrators of the 'History of the College' segment of the show. I have a freeze frame of you in my mind preparing to throw a frisbee we were playing with to pass the time at some stop. You are wearing your green suit, our tour uniform, and there is a huge grin on your face. You are young, you are beautiful and you are happy for ever.

And I don't use the word 'beautiful' lightly. You were a stunner. In *Lysistrata* at the Hopkins Center you spent much of your performance wearing only a loincloth. I recall thinking you were impossibly handsome, a compliment tempered only by my concern that you might catch cold.

When I went to Oxford, we lost touch for a few years. I got back in contact when you were starring in *Joseph and the Amazing Technicolor Dreamcoat* at the Brooklyn Academy of Music. By this time Tim Rice, who wrote the show with Andrew Lloyd Webber, had become one of my London friends. He and his brother Jo, their friend Mike Read and I had started work on a book called *The Guinness Book of British Hit Singles*. I thought it would be nifty to see you perform his work.

You were great. Once again you spent much of your time on stage in just a loincloth, although at least you occasionally got to put on the coat of many colours. The way you delivered 'Any Dream Will Do' convinced me this was a hit song in hiding, just waiting for the right recording. (In 1991 it did go to number one in Britain in a version by Jason Donovan. I know this because I just looked it up in the tenth edition of *Hit Singles*. We can never predict which things we do will last.)

On the subway back from Brooklyn we talked about the show – I remember vividly your bemused complaint about having to spend half the night with a microphone taped to your backside – and we caught up on the last five years. This wasn't two college kids talking about dreams any more, it was two young men starting to climb whatever it was we were climbing, leading to wherever it was we were going. I hadn't had a boyfriend yet, but I loved you. There, I said it. And why should I be afraid to say it? You loved me too. You let me know with a sweet mixture of affection and respect.

Of course I know what that respect was about. John Corwin was president of the class ahead of me in high school, and if I were to meet Dr Corwin today I would still defer to him as president of the senior class. I was already on WDCR, the college radio station, when you came to campus, so for all time it was as if I had played Shakespeare in Stratford.

I've always thought it isn't our feelings that cause us problems, it's what we do about them. We found ourselves at a crossroads while you were playing Joseph. Either we would become lovers or we would not. We didn't. I was too inexperienced to contemplate getting involved with some-one on the other side of an ocean. But I did write you immediately upon my return to London, and I remember the words with which my letter began. I wanted you to know then and there that I was devoted to you. You wrote me, too, and I want you to know here and now that I have kept all your letters.

Every time I went to New York after that we would meet. We often went to shows together. I'm afraid the moment that stays most vividly in my mind came when we went to see *Legs Diamond* with Robert. There was a point in the dreadful first half when the middle-aged leading lady complained, 'I'm too old for this crap!' which received nods and muttered assent from the audience. The star of that show, Peter Allen, later died of AIDS-related illnesses.

In the summer of 1983, we met at your place with nothing planned. This is, of course, what friends do: they get together, trusting they will enjoy each other's company, and choose an entertainment as it suits them at the moment. This casual approach is far more typical of American than English friends. I have often marvelled at the London habit of deciding what you are going to do a week or two beforehand, as if you might not want to see each other if there weren't a good enough reason. New

Yorkers often drop in or turn up on the doorstep on the spur of the moment, but, when this happens in London, it seems remarkably rude. This is because, even in an age of informality, the English retain a sense of privacy that is not only physical but also chronological. It is rude to get too close in either space or time. If you do happen to violate your friend's personal area, you will be forgiven, but you will sense your own gaffe as surely as a blindfolded man knows when he is standing in a hothouse.

There were no such reservations for us. I turned up at your apartment and we started throwing out suggestions as to what we could do. Again, as it is between friends, we did not care who came up with the winning idea. This was not a competition, it was a search. You had the best idea: since it was a brilliant summer's day, we should walk down Eighth Avenue and take in the International Food Festival. We could eat on the block with the Italian booths, sampling the efforts of various chefs. I needed no persuasion to lunch on the food of my forefathers, so we set off down Eighth.

Mayor Ed Koch was always capable of eliciting a combination of admiration and cynicism with his endless talent for self-promotion, but on this beautiful day he surprised even us. He appeared, seemingly from nowhere, like a drug-induced vision, leading a Puerto Rican school band marching down the avenue. The Mayor waved, not just politely, but enthusiastically, at the ethnics gathered around their respective stalls. They returned his greeting affectionately. This man had a common touch that helped him dominate New York City politics during the 1980s.

We had not yet eaten. Soon we would not be in the mood to eat. You were warmly greeted by a trio of friends, who engaged you in conversation, while I studied the offerings in the nearest food booths. I did not hear their words until they raised their voices to say goodbye.

'So we'll see you next Wednesday?' one of them asked innocently.

'Wednesday?' you replied, puzzled.

'John's funeral,' another friend explained.

'John?'

That much you managed to gasp. The second word, 'funeral', you didn't manage. Your three friends had assumed you had received the tragic news. You were actually unaware. Now the four of you entered a huddle in which the horrible details were exchanged. When you parted a second time, the farewells were far less hearty, verging on the solemn.

We were alone again in the middle of a crowd on Eighth Avenue. Your life had just been changed for ever. Mine was about to be.

'John and I were lovers in the late Seventies,' you told me. 'We hadn't been in touch for a while and I had no idea he was sick. I had no idea he would die.'

You paused and then shared a private thought, as if it was so strong you couldn't just think it, you had to state it aloud, too. 'He was the man I've loved most in my life so far.'

You hesitated again, for three or four seconds, and then said the natural thing. 'Excuse me, I've got to be alone for a minute.'

You walked back north to the next traffic light and then turned west toward Ninth. I stayed where I was, otherwise you wouldn't be able to find me when you came back. My head was spinning with portentous thoughts. No matter how close we were, you had never told me about John, and here was *bona fide* evidence of how we are able to compartmentalize our emotional lives, not informing someone who occupies one room who is living next door.

I moved beyond self-pity to consider your more serious predicament. I had by this time only deeply loved one man, Stephen, and I could not imagine how I would feel if he died, let alone if I were informed of his death as an aside in a casual conversation. I had reacted with fury when Stephen had been attacked by hooligans in a nightclub. If I could feel so strongly when he had merely been injured,

I could not begin to imagine how you were feeling after receiving sudden news of John's death.

I stood motionless as festive New Yorkers downed tacos, spring rolls and pizzas all around me. I wondered what I should do next. You had disappeared around the corner. What if you had kept going? What if I lost track of you? I decided I had to see where you were.

It did not take long. Upon reaching the traffic light where you had veered west, I looked in the direction of Ninth Avenue. I saw you sitting on a stoop, your head in your hands. You had retired to a side street to weep. Here the private nature of grief was demonstrated. A grown man was lost in sorrow in the midst of revels.

You did not need me to share this moment. I returned to our previous position and waited for your arrival. Presently, you came back.

'Excuse me, I needed that,' you said, and then continued. You had composed yourself, and you spoke forcefully. 'This is too much. Those friends of mine you just met told me that John died of this new disease no one knows anything about. People get these weird illnesses and just die. It's all over the city. They think it might be a new kind of cancer that gay people get, but nobody knows how you get it.' You paused and sighed. 'John's funeral is on Wednesday.'

David, I don't think I ever told you this, but that visit to the International Food Festival was one of the signal moments of my life. As when I lost my virginity or learned that Santa Claus didn't exist, there was no turning back. Many times I have wished I could reach back and recall the state of mind I was in before that sunny weekend afternoon, before I first learned about what we came to call AIDS. An impenetrable steel door blocks me from my own memories. I cannot bring back the time when we loved freely and fearlessly, though I know those years once existed.

Perhaps Kafka could have written our story. Here we

were, knowing the fatal consequences of a deed without knowing what the deed was. Without any idea of what we could and could not do safely, we seemed to divide into two groups: those who continued to do everything, thinking the disease was for other people, and those who did nothing, paralyzed by fear into thinking that even the slightest kiss might kill. Even the most paranoid could be forgiven their black fantasies, for here was what seemed like the first germ in history that targeted its victims on the basis of sexual orientation. Logic laughed at the possibility that a purely physical illness could be transmitted by emotional affinity, but what did logic have to do with it? The gay press, which I had previously ignored, but suddenly perused with a passion, was full of theories, including the notion that here, finally, was the swine flu Americans had feared during the 1970s.

I returned home to London a sobered man, determined to save my friends from the death that seemed to await them if they did not change their ways. Upon greeting my lodger, I issued a dramatic warning.

'I have seen the future and its name is death,' I announced to Chris. Compounding the solemnity of the occasion, I declared, 'From now on, there will be no fucking in this house.'

My friend could have been forgiven for thinking I had gone stark raving mad, but instead he chose to believe me and listened to my more measured explanation of what I had learned in New York. We agreed that, whatever was going on, full sex had to be dangerous because, if there were some sort of germ at work, anal intercourse would probably be a way it could get from one person to another. Kissing, on the other hand, had to be safe because, if kissing were a mode of transmission, everyone in New York would be dead. As for acts of affection in the range between kissing and fucking, we could only trust our instincts and be glad the disease was not yet rampant in England.

Many of our friends on the London scene had not yet heard of the illness, but most of those who had did not think it could affect them. They believed it was an American disease, particularly affecting New Yorkers. In retrospect this sounds preposterous, but no more so than to think that a virus could check out the sexual preference of a host before infecting it. Straight? You're safe. Gay? You're doomed. British? No worries. American? Dead man.

We were aghast at the indifference. Standing on the landing between the two floors of Heaven, London's biggest gay nightclub, watching hundreds of young and beautiful men, I confessed to Chris the extent of my distress.

'Take a good look at these guys,' I said. 'In five years, a quarter of them will be dead.'

As pretentious and condescending as my prediction was, it was probably an underestimate. But armed with what was for Britain advance notice of an impending health crisis, I was able to modify my behaviour and get two of my closest friends to do the same. Perhaps the three of us are alive today because of the chance encounter with three of your friends on Eighth Avenue.

During the decade from the early 1980s to the first years of the 1990s, we introduced each other to two of our partners. You were indignant at my choice of boyfriends, claiming after I had broken up with each of them that they had been gold diggers from the start and that I should protect myself from lovers who didn't actually love me. I was deeply touched that you should bother to feel so strongly about this, and that you would express your opinions to me, even at the threat of invoking my displeasure.

At this point I must pause for a second. I have suddenly remembered that on your trip to London in the late 1980s you slept in the very room in which I am writing this. I look over at the sofa-bed where you stayed for several nights. Of course, there is no evidence you were ever there. And can you believe this coincidence: above the sofa-bed hang my four original comic strips of *Henry*. The two men who as much as any represent my home city are recalled by items in my line of vision at this moment.

The first of your partners you introduced me to was also called Paul. Not until writing this sentence have I wondered whether you ever murmured intimacies with the name he and I shared. Of course you must have, numerous times. Now I wonder whether I should be jealous that, though spoken with my name, they were not directed at me.

My first meeting with Paul was at breakfast in the Cherry diner on Columbus Avenue, one of my brother Peter's favourite haunts until it was forced to close by rising rents that followed the gentrification of the Upper West Side. You and Paul were the picture of mutual infatuation that morning. I think it is fair to say that this charming crush did not grow into mature love, because after a relatively short period of time you had become good friends rather than exclusive lovers. I heard both of you say catty things about the other, indicating that you cared, but were not fulfilled. Paul moved to Los Angeles and worked in show business behind the scenes. The last time I saw him was when he was in London on a short trip. He was now a beautifully proportioned Californian, a far cry from the wispy New Yorker I had first met. He had found and was enjoying a new life on the West Coast.

'I finally figured it out,' he said just before I let him out of my car at Lancaster Gate tube station. 'The reason men in Los Angeles are so much better developed than Londoners. In LA it's so warm people are showing off their bodies all the time, so they work out like crazy to look good. Here it's too cold, they never take their clothes off, they don't care about it that much.'

Having presented his body-building thesis, Paul gave me a hug and a kiss, and asked me to see him when I was next in LA. I promised I would, but I never got a chance to keep that promise. He died of AIDS the following year. He had looked so good it never occurred to me he might leave us so quickly.

I didn't get to see every show you were in. Who could? One musical, *Oh Brother!*, lasted only one performance. Still, it was Broadway. Even the flops you appeared in were of a higher class than many people's successes. *Ball Four*, based on Jim Bouton's successful memoir, was a television failure, but at least it was prime time and, most impressive to a baseball fanatic like myself, you got to act the part of a ballplayer! You were definitely moving up, but the public didn't know it yet. They were seeing your face without knowing the name, as when your handsome mug appeared advertising vodka in every subway car in the city.

Then things turned right for you, like all the rows of a slot machine coming up cherries at the same time. You found fulfillment with Robert. Here was the kind of relationship most people hope for, but never find. Indeed, many people never even approach a partnership of such quality. They assume, because they do not near it themselves, that it cannot exist. You and Robert were proof that a marriage of soulmates is not a fantasy.

I almost expected that on my first visit to New York after you two got together I would find you both with red ears. They should have been burning from the way you spoke about each other. I immediately approved of your new choice of partner: a man of your own generation in a business unrelated to ours was probably the best choice you could have made. Of course, choice had nothing to do with it. You simply adored each other and had to be together.

In the interests of keeping the relationship both intimate and fresh, you expressed the desire to spend part of your time living with Robert and some in a place of your own. To that end we planned on buying an apartment together, to give you a place to be on your own when you sought solitude and me a regular place to stay when I was in the city.

During the 1980s I had taken to checking in at the Plaza, but the changes initiated by the Trumps were not to my liking. All the security men standing around with visible earpieces reminded me of secret police, as if guests would be punished if they stepped out of line. Jackets and ties became required for breakfast in the Edwardian Room, where for many years I had traditionally enjoyed the first meal of the first day of every visit to New York. No more. When you are on vacation, the last thing you want is to dress up for breakfast.

A happy alternative to the Plaza was provided by a great friend and her husband. This trusting duo allowed me a regular bed in their Fifth Avenue apartment. I had comfort and luxury without fearing I would be arrested by the concierge.

During the late 1980s you and I talked often about the toll AIDS was taking in the theatre. One evening at Joe Allen we noted the death of a playwright of twenty-nine, who had not only died young but also had his only major musical savaged by the press.

'Of course a lot of these people don't take care of themselves,' you asserted. Not knowing them personally, I could not disagree. 'They do drugs and they party. If you have the virus, but live a healthy life, you're more likely to stay healthy. Eat the right things, sleep good hours, that kind of thing.'

I had to wonder if you were making a veiled reference to your own health. With the directness close friends allow each other, I asked if you had been tested. You said you had not and would not be. Since there was no effective treatment for the disease, there was not yet any medical point in knowing your status. Besides, the emotional consequences of a positive diagnosis might be too upsetting. You were taking as good care of yourself as you could. You even insisted that we walk on the sunny side of the street, a habit I picked up from you. As long as you lived in a healthy way, you were more likely to stay healthy than if you stressed yourself with knowledge you didn't need.

This idea of 'knowledge you didn't need', a new concept to information junkies like myself, was one that had found favour in the London gay community as well as in New York. You had your own sense of discretion about HIV. You never spoke to me about being HIV positive, not in so many words, ever, but you happily talked around it.

You never told me you had AIDS, but you let me know. One afternoon, at 1.30, I was amazed to hear from you out of the blue, explaining that it would not be possible to go ahead with our plans to buy an apartment together. Your career had become financially uncertain and you could not commit to such an expense.

I couldn't believe it. It was 8.30 in the morning in New York. You would never have made an overseas call at that time of day unless you felt a real urgency, and telling me you couldn't get an apartment with me was hardly vital. I was in London, after all, not New York, and hardly in the position to go house-hunting on the West Side. The news could have waited for a letter or my next trip to the States. Anyway, far from being in decline, your career was in its ascendancy. Your compulsion to phone me at that time of the day made me conclude you were actually telling me something completely different. You would not be able to share an apartment with me because you weren't going to be able to be with me. Either you had received literal medical news or you had accepted within yourself that you had little time left.

I thought back to our walk down Eighth Avenue in 1983. I recalled how, when you heard the news of the death of your special friend, you had retired to a side street to weep. I now wondered if you were crying not just for him but also for yourself.

You may have had limited time left, but you made the most of it. You capped your career with starring roles in *Chess* and *Grand Hotel*, earning Tony nominations for both. *Chess* got to me the most. Because the lyricist was my old pal Tim Rice, I had followed this project from its inception. Tim and I had been chatting at a reception for Abba in a London restaurant when Bjorn and Benny entered the building. Before they reached us, Bjorn told a reporter that their next project was going to be a musical with Tim Rice.

'I guess I've got to do it now,' Tim said with his usual understatement. *Chess* was official. I felt the resulting album, which preceded the West End staging, was the best musical recording of the 1980s. When the show was presented at the Prince Edward Theatre in London, the Swedish star Tommy Körnberg brought the house down with his first act closer, 'Anthem'. I was crazy about this song and even recommended it to Placido Domingo when he asked me what stage songs I thought he should cover on a future album. (I'm not surprised the great man did not take my advice; he certainly never asked if I thought the Three Tenors should record 'My Way'.)

It was delicious when you were cast as the Russian grand master. Tim had always said you were the best Joseph he had ever seen in America, so I knew you would have his support. You were very apprehensive about the reaction of director Trevor Nunn, who had made such a name for himself in America with *Nicholas Nickleby* and *Cats*, but you needn't have worried. He was enthusiastic about your performance. The only thing concerning the New York production you had to worry about was being knocked over by one of the moving pillars.

I was thrilled to fly in for opening night. To make it sweeter, Binky Rockwell, our great friend from Dartmouth, came in from Minnesota. We joined you in celebrations at the opening night party at the United Nations. It was surreal, of course, that the General Assembly building, which represented the best hope of humanity for peace and progress, should be making up some of its budgetary short-fall by leasing its facilities at night to show business. It was also odd to see, as an adult at a party, a structure which had seemed so imposing and impressive when I was a child.

The greatest delight of *Chess*, the indelible moment, was your performance of 'Anthem'. All other artists had left the stage, giving the Russian the chance to make a dramatic impact with his solo. This you did. It was thrilling for me to be back in the city of my birth, watching my great New York friend sing a lyric written by my great London friend. In a geographically divided life such as mine, we are given few moments of unity. Your version of 'Anthem', which stole the show, was such an occasion for me. Thank you for it.

You got your Tony nomination. Michael Crawford won for *Phantom*, but beating him in that would have been like keeping Elvis Presley out of number one in 1957. You revisited *Chess* triumphantly when you organized a charity concert performance of the original cast in Carnegie Hall. I came in for that one too. Call me a *Chess* groupie! And why not? I'd kissed the leading man more often than Judy Kuhn! (J for Joke, Robert, this is a joke.)

Shortly thereafter you took the John Barrymore role in Tommy Tune's musical production of *Grand Hotel*. You were the poster boy on this one, and what a poster. There was hunky David on virtually every bus in New York City. You also loomed large over Times Square. This was really one for the memoirs, I thought. I'd seen Times Square celebrity billboards from Sam Cooke to Lena Zavaroni, and here was my buddy setting thousands of theatregoing hearts aflutter. Had Lena Zavaroni's friends felt this proud? They probably never made it over from Scotland.

Grand Hotel was another triumph for you, and you got another Tony nomination. I was amused that audiences cannot realize how physical many stage performances are. Not only did you have to dodge Stonehenge in *Chess*, you also had to climb all over the *Grand Hotel* set like a spider. Yet, if you did these technical things well, which you did, the effect was to be so ordinary no one noticed you were doing anything.

The real challenge was doing the Charleston with Michael Jeter. The first stretch, of course, was learning the routine. I watched this scene with a combination of pride and amusement. I could not possibly imagine you ever doing this kind of dance in real life. Just trying to picture it has me in stitches.

The major achievement was doing this strenuous scene when you were unwell. The London equivalent was Ian Charleson carrying on with *Hamlet* at the National Theatre when he was in his final months. For a period you had to come out of the show, and it was at this time you started speaking to me frankly and specifically about your ailments. You were determined to return to the cast, as any trouper would be, but you had to face the challenge of being talked about while ill. Rumours spread that you did, in fact, have AIDS, although it was pneumonia which was given as the specific reason for taking a break. It is one thing to be 'out' as a gay man and another to be a poster boy for AIDS when employment is at risk. You faced both the disease and the talk, and returned heroically to dance on in *Grand Hotel*.

The last time I saw you in London was when you and Robert were stopping over on your return to New York from Zurich. You had gone to Switzerland to try an unusual form of therapy. A generous person would call the treatment experimental; cynics would consider it quackery. To be honest, I can't remember what form it took, other than it involved large amounts of some fruit derivative, though whether it was apricots or apples didn't matter to me. I was just glad you'd found some hope. Whether it was optimism supported by science or wishful thinking born of novelty, I was glad to find you in good spirits.

What I was not prepared for was your physical weakness. I met you at the lobby elevator at the Savoy Hotel and had to walk you into the restaurant. A side effect of your treatment was that you had lost feeling in the soles of your feet.

In every incidence of AIDS involving friends I have known for years there is a moment when the enormity of the situation makes itself evident. This isn't just a dear person fallen ill. This is a loved one in decline. The contrast between the long-held image of the healthy person and the new reality is so immense it is shocking. I've adjusted within moments, and there will never again during the course of the illness be a moment quite as surprising, but for those seconds I'm stunned.

You can appreciate my desire to disbelieve as I physically supported my always active friend, an athlete superior to myself in school and university, an actor who had danced vigorously on the stage, even when ill. Did you know, David, this was the moment I could no longer hope you would not fall, that the question was not how much fruit essence we could give you to keep you going, but how could the next eighteen months or so be made most bearable for you?

I even questioned my eighteen-month estimate when we sat down for lunch and you casually recited your latest litany of illnesses. You mentioned and dismissed an eye problem that I had just read in the *International Herald Tribune* was associated with a life expectancy of between six and twelve months. When you had drunk your fruit juice to make a midday pill go down easier, you had to retire from the restaurant because the food odours were so over-powering. Robert and I went back to your room and set out on a mission to get what you really wanted for lunch: a plain chicken sandwich. No sauce, no salad, no side orders, just a simple chicken sandwich.

This was a far more challenging assignment than it sounded. We could have tried room service, but thought that would take too long, so off into Covent Garden we went. It quickly became apparent that all the chicken sandwiches sold in the market and in stores were pre-made and included some sort of cheese or salad in addition to the meat. This was a comic scene, two middle-aged men hustling through the side streets of WC2 in search of a plain chicken sandwich. Never in my life have I been so frustrated by a few pieces of cheese.

Fortunately I had been to Joe Allen that week and had a very good chicken and cheese sandwich that was on their current menu. Since the London Joe Allen is the place where I have eaten more meals in my life than any place other than my own home, always getting a friendly greeting, I knew that whoever was on the door would be receptive to my request for that wonderful sandwich, hold the cheese. It was appropriate we go to Joe's anyway, since you and I had eaten in the New York restaurant and Robert knew it too. As expected, the staff were happy to take our unusually basic order of a plain chicken sandwich to go.

Your partner and I were not prepared for the next few moments. We had been so busy rushing around looking for your lunch that it never occurred to us there would be a few minutes of complete inactivity while we waited for the order to be prepared. As our adrenalin levels dropped, we had a moment to contemplate the gravity of what was happening.

Robert sobbed. These were not tiny tears. His eyes did not grow moist, his orbs did not turn dewy. He *sobbed*, big balls of water that rolled down his face. Here he was, a successful self-employed businessman in a tie, standing in the middle of a popular restaurant on a Sunday afternoon, unable and unwilling to conceal his elemental grief.

'Paul,' he said, 'what can I do? I love him.'

The question was not meant to be answered. Robert and I were visiting the same emotional territory, walking as lover and old friend through land that was dark and cold, oblivious to whoever might have been watching him weep, oblivious to everyone except the waiter who a few minutes later gave us a bag containing a plain chicken sandwich.

We returned to the Savoy, where, thank God, you had the appetite to eat it. It was then and there that I knew I had to give my life's speech, to say everything I would ever want to say to you, in the company of your beloved Robert, before it was too late. You certainly weren't expecting it and might not even have recognized it as the declaration it was, but I had to make it and I am glad I did.

'David,' I began, 'there have been times in the last fifteen years when I have wondered what it would have been like if you and I had tried to become a couple. I realize now that it doesn't matter at all whether we did or not, because I could not love you more than I do today anyway, and you could not have a more loving or devoted partner than you do in Robert. He is perfect for you.'

'I know,' you said. And that was that.

Except that, in the months which followed, Robert proved it again and again, every minute of every day, in all the little ways only someone who has tended a slowly dying person knows. Occasionally you would tell me on the phone of the latest medical catastrophe to befall you, but as they became numerous, they seemed to become nuisances rather than calamities. A new illness doesn't seem so serious when you've already got three of them. Your body became a medical gymnasium, as happens when doctors prescribe multiple therapies on the same person, and Robert was with you performing the sensitive daily procedures that enhanced your intimacy.

I altered my customary Christmas vacation pattern. Usually I would work through Christmas Eve and then fly to New York, not realizing the pre-holiday torment of radio and TV pre-recordings was concluded until I was on the plane. But this year you were flying down to Florida with Robert to spend Christmas with your family in a reunion full of symbolism and – yes, I'll say it – joy. It might seem macabre to someone who hasn't had this experience that a holiday with a terminally ill person at the table can be joyous. But you knew, I know you did, that to go out with a Christmas during which you were fully reconciled to your parents, with Robert welcomed as a full member of the family, was one of the greatest achievements of your achievement-filled life. Recognizing this, I flew to New York the week before Christmas and visited you before you went to Florida. No seer had to tell me this would be the last time I saw you.

You were so ill, confined to bed and very weak. And yet, when I entered the room, you rose from the bed and walked over to greet me, embracing me as warmly and as tightly as you had on Park Lane in London or Central Park West in New York. (I never told you, but I preferred hugging you with my head over your left shoulder rather than your right; we seemed to fit together better that way.)

I was as astonished by this as if you had performed the decathlon. You weren't supposed to have the strength for this. I thought of Olivier playing King Lear for television. So weak in the wings that some crew members wondered if he would get through the performance, he strode on stage carrying his dead daughter as if she were a bag of feathers. There is a secret strength we gather for moments when we want it, and you summoned it then.

We are, all of us, prone to self-doubt. We cannot help but wonder if we mean as much to our dear ones as they do to us. Yet there are times when we are presented with evidence so overwhelming we have to surrender our insecurities. When you got out of your sickbed and crossed the room to embrace me, I had to yield whatever final suspicions I might have sheltered. We really were, for each other and to each other, loving friends.

You performed the same stunt again after Robert and a female friend had served a dietetically current dinner. As I left to return to the other side of the park, you rose to see me out and hugged me tightly. You spoke with enthusiasm of your family Christmas in Florida and your planned concert at the 92nd Street Y. You looked forward to the next time we would meet and wished me a good holiday. I looked at you, taking a mental picture of the moment, and wished you a Merry Christmas. I said goodbye to Robert, gave you a goodnight kiss and got into the elevator, thinking on the way down to 68th Street that I had just seen my dear David for the last time.

I was right. You did heroically struggle on for nearly three more months. You managed to make it to the night you had looked forward to, the concert at the 92nd Street Y. Although you were physically unable to sing songs in succession, you cleverly called upon female singers you had befriended during your career to alternate numbers with you, as if in musical conversation.

And then you made it to another milestone. You had lobbied for ages for an original cast recording of *Grand Hotel* to be made. Finally a deal was done and dates scheduled. You went to the first session with Robert, got into the studio and, in a matter of moments, collapsed. You died in his arms. He felt your spirit leave your body.

Boy, did you know how to leave the stage. You died, as they say, with your boots on, in the recording studio where you wanted to be on a project you helped to make possible. And you passed on in the arms of the person who meant the most to you, giving him the suitable reward of tending to you in your final moment, as he had cared for you in so many moments. You were a class act to the very end.

You probably saw the memorial service. You saw Linda Lavin get quite emotional about your hard work for your emergency shelter charity, and you saw Michael Jeter, your Charleston partner in *Grand Hotel*, grow even more emotional. You must have seen the video tribute paid you by Trevor Nunn, who sounded so complimentary, so effusive and so upset, all at the same time, that someone who didn't know him might have thought he had decided to become an actor rather than a director. But I have to tell you, I ran into Trevor in the Green Room at TV-am in London, and when I informed him I had seen his contribution to the service, he grew visibly distressed and launched a similar salute, telling me how broken up he was that he wasn't going to be able to do the projects he wanted with you and share the social time he enjoyed with you. And you were afraid he wouldn't like you at the

Chess audition! Ha! I found myself thinking, wait a minute here, David was my friend first, but we were called to the sofa and that was that. On another occasion I found myself sitting next to Tommy Tune and during the commercial break I told him you had been my friend. He expressed his sorrow, but it seemed more general, with regard to his entire roster of lost cast members, than to you in particular.

The rest you know better than I. We're doing OK. Robert suffered terribly, as you wished he wouldn't, but knew he would, though he has gone on to great distinction in his career and has regained what we call, for lack of a better expression, perspective. In emotional terms perspective isn't the angle at which you look at something, it's what you look at. Your absence, for this is what your death literally means to us, will never be satisfactory. That you were robbed of years of happiness with Robert, that you were denied Broadway roles you would have played and Tony awards you would have won will never be OK. No perspective will make what is wrong right. But, by gradually concentrating on other aspects of life and other types of relationships, Robert has come through. You must be so relieved to know he has made it.

As for me, the city has been so much emptier without you. You were the only person, other than my brother Peter, who I saw at least twice every time I came to town, and there has been a void without you. I miss your romantic advice, even if it almost always consisted of some variation of 'could do better'. The abyss was made deeper when Tyler Gatchell took his leave shortly after you, suddenly and from a completely different illness. You guys are probably looking at us right now and reviewing our day-to-day performances.

Don't believe the clichés. Time does not heal old wounds, it just dresses them. Gradually you do make a couple of new friends and you do reinforce some old friendships. No one lost is replaced, but at least other people are found.

Now comes the moment I've dreaded. Now comes the end of this note. It has been a year and a half since I started writing you. During that time several other dear people have been lost to AIDS, including my young friend Ashford, my great colleague Kenny and my precious PA, Terry. I've been able to write a letter to Terry – you can read it, it's on page 129 – and I've eulogized Kenny in public. I've spoken about Ashford more than once with his mother. But I haven't wanted to come back and finish this. At first I thought it might be because you are my oldest friend who has died, but that doesn't explain it. After all, the whole of my life, even as a child, people were popping off around me – strange, I know, but several children died in school, and seven of the customers on my paper route passed away, anything to avoid payment.

No, I haven't wanted to finish for the same reason I didn't want to start. I've been spooked at how we were two takes on the same theme: Catholic boys from Fairfield County who went to Dartmouth and followed careers in show business. It's almost as if every time we met from the mid-1970s on we were comparing notes on what might have happened to each other had we followed a different road. Of course, at this point, reality taps me on the shoulder and reminds me that I can't sing, but I'm not claiming we literally could have had each other's careers. I'm just saying we're cut from the same cloth, chips off the same block, pieces of the same puzzle. We overlapped, David. Saying goodbye to you for good means part of me is gone for good too.

Thank God the part of you that is in me is still here. Believe me, it always will be. You gave me so much – hope that we can overcome early emotional difficulties, knowledge that with the right person we can build a successful partnership, inspiration that we can achieve what seem like impossible career goals.

And don't forget: thanks to you, I walk on the sunny side of the street.

STEPHEN

I believe in love at first sight. I believe because I met you.

I was attending a reception in a Mayfair club to launch the 1980 Diana Ross album *Diana*, the one with 'Upside Down' and 'I'm Coming Out' on it. It was a great album, but a lousy reception. With neither Miss Ross nor any other artist present, there seemed little reason to linger after saying hello, then goodbye, to my colleagues.

On my way out I passed through the public bar. I saw you out of the corner of my right eye.

My first thought was: that man is going to become an important part of my life.

My second thought was: I can't believe I just thought something so corny.

My third thought was: yes, it's corny, but it's true.

I had to meet you. But how? You were in a group of revellers, clearly friends on a night out, and I had no idea how to interrupt. I couldn't ask your opinion of *Diana*, you hadn't been in the reception. I had no way of knowing that you, like Miss Ross, would that night be 'coming out'.

Fate and fame intervened. If anyone ever asks the benefits of being publicly known, I truthfully reply that they include good seats at restaurants and concerts, admission to clubs, and that's about it. I should include that being a minor celebrity helped me win an introduction to my first boyfriend.

One of your party, bless him, bless him, bless him, was a fan of mine. He came over to talk to me. Can you believe it? Here I am sweating it out over how to go and talk to you, and one of your pals makes a beeline for me. I politely answered his interview questions for about three minutes before casually adding to the end of a reply, 'And who are your friends?' We – and two more of your university classmates – were introduced.

Classmates! Students! A bit of an age difference here, I thought, I must go carefully – not because you might be under twenty-one and I was afraid of the law since the discriminatory age of consent never even entered my mind, but because I might look a bit stupid at the age of thirty chatting up a heterosexual who was only twenty. I was always more afraid of being impolite than being convicted.

You seemed to enjoy the conversation, but you did not wish to take it in a personal direction while in the company of your friends, with whom, it turned out, you studied at a university within two hours of London. Realizing that I was not going to pull someone who was definitely in straight company, I said my goodbyes and retreated to a table near the exit. I gave myself five minutes to think of a strategy to get you alone. After that, I would leave.

I didn't think of a strategy and I didn't leave. You came over to me. You left your friends for a moment and sat right down at my table.

'How are things, Paul?' you asked with the ear-to-ear grin that would become your trademark. I dutifully recited my latest career commitments.

'No, I mean, how are things with you, Paul?' Here was your second trademark: the mischievous glint in your eye. 'Come on, I've had my gay times, you know.'

I can't recall if we broke the land speed record to my apartment, but in my memory now we made it there in a nanosecond. You were both affectionate and passionate, so much so that I was surprised the next morning when, upon leaving, you asked, 'Will I see you again?'

You mean you do this with men and don't see them again?

Of course I saw you again. And after that I wanted to see you again, again. But I didn't hear from you.

'Tell me about it!' your average smitten suitor might cry. Everyone has been in the situation where they're longing to hear from someone and can't phone them. In your case you lived in a hall of residence, and the odds against either catching you in or getting someone to answer the phone in the first place were astronomical.

How much did I love you? Part One: I drove to see you, uninvited. I never do that. I don't mean I never do anything uninvited, although that's true as well; I mean I never drive out of London. Although I love driving around the big city, moving in and out of traffic like an exercise in vector analysis, I grow extremely agitated on motorways. I have had several acquaintances die in highway accidents and I cannot recapture my automotive innocence. When I was a teenager, I used to motor up and down the East Coast of the United States with abandon (I will resist using the word 'gay' in this context), but knowing that any driver could become part of what the public service announcements used to call 'the carnage on our nation's highways' has put a damper on my enthusiasm. Nonetheless, to see you, I drove out of town.

That was hazardous enough, at least from my point of view. What was risky by any account was that I didn't know where your hall of residence was and how I would ever find your room. Here was a situation with two possible extreme outcomes. In one I find you and declare my love; you reciprocate and we live happily ever after. In the other scenario a Radio 1 disc jockey stumbles around campus looking for his two-night stand and gets a reputation for annoying college students.

I found the hall and found your room, both without difficulty. The only problem was that your room-mate was in and you weren't! How do you pretend you're just dropping by for a chat when you live miles away and never drop by for any reason? Once again the benefits of fame came to the fore, and your room-mate, satisfied by the explanation that we had met at a party and uninterested in why I might be in your town, contented himself with a few questions of the interview variety. He then excused himself, having previously made an appointment, but said you would be back soon and that I should make myself comfortable.

With nothing else to do, I took a nap. I awoke when you came into the room.

With your girlfriend.

'Paul!' you exclaimed, as if surprised. No wonder – you were surprised! 'Meet Judy.'

You could have knocked Judy over with a feather. What is a Radio 1 deejay doing in my boyfriend's room, her raised eyebrows asked.

It was then that I learned what a charmer you were. You smoothly explained to her I had just dropped by for a visit and, if she would only wait in the room for a half hour or so, your evening together would continue.

Unable to use your room or for that matter anybody else's, we got into my car and drove around the campus. This was hardly my idea of a fun evening, particularly since I had already spent a substantial part of it behind the wheel, but it was the only way to get some privacy.

You were remarkably frank, I give you credit. You told me you were bisexual and that Judy was your girlfriend. You also said you had assumed I would not wish to see you because you were not good for me.

'Paul,' you said in complete earnest, 'I'm a bad person. You don't want me.'

'Stephen,' I said, trying to keep my hands on the wheel and not on you, 'please don't assume you know how I feel. I do want you. And I cannot accept that you are a bad person.'

'Believe me,' you insisted. 'I'm a bad person. I will hurt you.'

'Do you want to?' I asked.

'Of course not,' you answered.

'Do you want to try staying together?'

'Of course.'

'Then let's try.'

And so we tried, for three and a half years. Shortly thereafter you moved into my London apartment. We went for a long weekend in Paris for our private honeymoon. I'm not ashamed to say that my fondest memory of the stay is of the last night when, while I was tired and not contemplating romance, you reached over to me. At that moment you were not hung up on your sexual identity, you were not embarrassed that you loved me, you were just grateful – not that I was about to pay the bill, grateful that we had managed to take three days out of our lives and devote them exclusively to each other. I hope you remember our afternoon in Versailles – I've still got the photos if you need reminding – and I almost hope you've forgotten the day it just kept raining. We would escape a downpour at one Métro station only to emerge into another cloudburst at a second. I remember how amused you were that the breakfast tray was brought into the room each morning by a young Frenchwoman. You wondered what she was thinking went on between us. I wondered if you fancied her. I thought the whole scenario was out of *Women in Love*.

I was proud of you, getting on at university, and you were proud of me. You came as my guest to the House of Commons when we had our launch party for *Hits of the Seventies*. This was the only party in history that got more press with each day following, for this was when Elton John was rumoured to have sat in the Speaker's Chair and the Chancellor of the Duchy of Lancaster had his tie tugged by the American Indian from the Village People. Perhaps it would have received even more press if we had pointed out that one of the authors had brought along his twenty-year-old (and hence illegal) boyfriend. The preposterously unjust age of consent for two men needed to be equalized with that for heterosexuals. When we began, you, though the younger partner, had had more sexual experience with men than I and, when you wanted love, you didn't consent, you insisted.

I was so happy that I had for the first time in my life set up home with someone. You had Judy, then several women, then Judy again, but I didn't mind. They weren't men. If you had entertained another boyfriend, I would have gone through the roof, but I was, I still believe, your only man. The women I could handle. I even accepted the occasional visit from a male teacher with whom you had had an affair in your early adolescence. It didn't bother me that you had been sexually precocious; I was relieved I could in no way be accused of having corrupted you.

One thing happened to prove I was not as saintly as the nuns who had taught me in Sunday School liked to think. One morning you appeared at the foot of my bed at 6.30. You were wearing my raincoat. It was covered in your blood. The previous night you had borrowed the coat to go to a nightclub in the West End. In the early morning hours a young tough playing pool thought he saw you ogling his girlfriend. He and two friends put billiard balls in a sock and beat you with it.

As I held you in my arms while you told me the story, I was filled with deep feelings. Naturally I was relieved you were now safe and of course I was aware of my transcendent love for you. But I was also extremely glad the club was only yards from a police station and that your assailants had been arrested. I was full of such fury I knew that, if they had not been apprehended, I would have taken the weeks or months necessary to track them down and, one by one, beat them brutally.

I had never before realized I was capable of violence. I had abhorred the idea of service in the Vietnam War, but my objections had not been put to the test since I was assigned a high number in Nixon's draft lottery. I was always against the death penalty as administered by society, but had philosophically toyed with the possible appropriateness of vigilantism. While at Oxford I had met a classmate's sister, an intelligent and beautiful young woman who, at the age of twenty-one, was raped and murdered by an intruder in her Georgetown apartment. Although the presumed culprit had been caught, the evidence had not been sufficient to convict and he had been set free. My friend's father was so overwhelmed he had to leave his position in government and take a business job in New York, for he knew that, if he remained in Washington, he would track down and kill his daughter's murderer. This, on an admittedly smaller scale, is what I felt when I gently kissed your bloodied and puffed face. How much did I love you? Part Two: I would have thrashed anyone who hurt you.

We did have one fight ourselves over a third man, but fortunately it was only verbal. We were at a party at John's country house and became separated, as couples tend to do in large social gatherings. I was astonished when I walked into the bedroom that was functioning as the *de facto* cloakroom: you were lying on the bed underneath a prominent London restaurateur. Resting on the bed, I could understand, but lying on your back being caressed by one of my alleged friends was more than I could take. You resisted my request to leave the room with me.

I returned to the party visibly shaken. Freddie Mercury asked what was wrong. When I told him you were in a clinch with clubland's leading caterer, he gathered a posse of pals and stormed into the bedroom, routing the offender. My hero! Freddie had my eternal gratitude. You, on the other hand, were not so impressed. You yelled as we walked to the car that I had embarrassed you in front of our friends. I replied that, the way I recalled it, you had embarrassed me. Freddie would not have led his charge had you not been indiscreet.

I underestimated the strength of your feelings. A few hundred yards out of John's driveway you demanded I stop the car. You were not going to go home with me. I could not bear the acrimony and brought my little Fiat to a halt. You got out, slamming the door. I moved down the road, entertaining dreadful fantasies of you returning to the arms of your suitor.

Just before the curve in the road I looked in my rear-view mirror and saw you. You hadn't moved a step. You hadn't intended to go back to him after all, you were merely mad at me. Now you were a lonely young man with neither his lover nor his seducer, standing in the middle of a country lane late at night miles from London. I drove back to you, opened the car door and asked you to get in. You did. We went home.

This was the first important example of your tendency to project your own feelings on to me. You were humiliated that you'd been discovered in a compromising position and furious events had taken the turn they had. You translated your rage at the situation into anger at me.

For two and a half of our three and a half years I had no difficulty in accommodating your love life with women. Indeed, I so wanted you to be happy I even partially funded your night life with them. You kept saying you would repay the money you borrowed to entertain them at nightclubs, some of which I had introduced you to, but you never did and never have. We kept a running account so we knew how much was involved, and I'm afraid to say that you still owe me £1,300 at 1983 prices. That might not seem much, but £1,300 was a measurable percentage of my annual income in 1983. It was a pitiful indication of my affection for you that I paid out of my own pocket so you could impress other lovers.

But, sigh, this is what we do. I was the older of the two of us and had more resources. I felt it fell to me to make this contribution. I've always had the tendency to believe in 'the project', the long-term survival of a partnership, whatever the short-term difficulties. This has not been a fashionable approach to relationships in the past fifteen years, particularly with persons under thirty-five accustomed to the rapid channel-changing of television remote controls and the split-second editing of MTV. I have frequently been amazed by individuals seemingly in love one day and out of touch the next, as if they had come upon the advertising junction after *News at Ten* and decided to turn to *Newsnight*.

I hung in with you. Boy, did I hang in. During our last year things were very difficult. Instead of being increasingly happy to ally yourself with me in public, you grew more and more insistent upon presenting yourself as a heterosexual. All my friends were telling me I had to leave you. Dear old Freddie told me I deserved better. I arrived at the moment when the mind knows it will have to make a change as soon as the heart allows.

I'm afraid you made it easy. On more than one occasion you became rowdy when drunk. You came home one night to find someone sleeping in the living-room and you forced him to leave. You came into my room and nearly overturned the bed in your rage. I got a call from my unlucky visitor the next day saying he wasn't going to associate with me if I insisted on living with someone so aggressive.

Another morning, after you had invited friends over for drinks, I rose to find the furniture in the living-room in disarray. When I enquired which of your pals had gotten unruly, you couldn't remember and phoned one of them. You were told, to our mutual horror, that it was, in fact, you who had started throwing things around and they who had fled.

On a third occasion, while you were entertaining a woman, I had a male friend over. I asked you to turn the washing machine off before you went to bed, and you went wild. You accused me of trying to embarrass you in front of a woman and you attacked me. I had to pull you into the bathroom so the brawl could be held outside the gaze of our guests. I felt like United Nations forces in a defensive war: I had no desire to hurt you, but I had to do my best to avoid being hurt by you. You zapped me one on the nose and bent one of my fingers back very painfully, but I managed to pin you like an upright wrestler until you had finally grown tired of the struggle. When we emerged from the bathroom, I discovered my guest had taken refuge in my room and was cowering by the bed, afraid your rampage might become directed at him. He, too, never visited the flat again.

It had to end when I started hanging around socially with Chris Hamill. In the beginning, since his group's first single had not yet been released, he was not a public figure, and you merely treated him with polite frostiness. When 'Too Shy' exploded, however, going to number one in February 1983, you could not contain your dislike. One moment when the three of us were standing outside the kitchen is etched on my memory. You are smiling your trademark smile, but it is frozen on your face. There is hatred in your eyes.

You were jealous of Chris. Despite my insistence that he and I were not a couple, you were constantly suspicious that we were lovers. Of course the tabloid press voiced the same sensational contention, but their reporters had no idea that I already had a boyfriend, mainly because they never asked. You knew I was devoted to you – or at least, after three and a half years, you should have known.

I would have happily lived with and loved you for ever, but you were not interested in being a couple. You didn't want us to be faithful lovers because you wanted to have the women you desired. On the other hand, you got upset not only when I saw another man but also when it looked like I might be seeing one. You couldn't accept that, when I did take another lover, it was only because you were engaged with women and had made yourself unavailable to me. In short, you were possessive of our relationship, even though you wished you didn't want it, and you resented any potential intruders.

I had to make a change. I feared that one day, perhaps soon, you would have an outburst, and that really would make the papers.

I bought myself a house in Islington. I knew I couldn't take you with me. You were growing so distant from me that I knew we had to finish.

One morning you came into my room and I told you I would be moving without you. I was in bed; you were on the couch by the window. When I broke the news, you were disconsolate. You tried to persuade me to change my mind, to convince me you would be a new man and would never be violent again. When I said this was easier said than done, you crawled into bed next to me, held me and cried. You begged me to take you with me.

I've had easier moments in my life, Stephen. I wished you had shown me this tenderness months earlier. But I knew your personality was unlikely to be altered just because I wanted it to be. We can offer someone the opportunity to change, but we can't make them change, and in the time we lived together I did not change you. I couldn't make you any more comfortable with the homosexual part of your nature than you had been when I met you. Perhaps you were even less comfortable.

As the next few years went by I saw you only occasionally, when you accepted an invitation to my annual birthday party. There you would be safe in mixed company, not having to face the prospect of seduction or intimate conversation. Then you stopped attending. An unplanned and inconceivable humiliation followed.

One evening we arrived simultaneously from different directions at the door of Orso in Covent Garden. To my astonishment you refused to walk down the stairs into the restaurant with me. When I phoned you that week to find out why, you told me that you were meeting business contacts and you didn't want them to think you were gay.

Paranoia central, pal! Why would anyone think a person was gay just because he was having a conversation with someone of the same sex? Perhaps you thought everyone in the country knew I was gay and would only talk to another man if I were having an affair with him. (This, of course, would not only severely restrict my activities at work but also on the Regent's Park Softball Club and with fellow vintage comic collectors.)

We began to speak only once a year. You wouldn't invite me to see you and avoided meetings. On one occasion when we did dine, you told me that, when we had been together, you couldn't bear being with me in public. You had been sure everyone thought you were there as my toy boy. I pointed out this was certainly not my own feeling, and you agreed it was only your own perception, but it was your fear and you were entitled to it. I asked one of your gay friends who you did meet regularly why you had blanked me and he said, 'Can't you see? You're the one person who brings it out in him.'

In other words, with me and only with me you had feelings you considered homosexual. You didn't want to be homosexual. Therefore, if you did not see me, you would not be.

This is a classic case of blaming the messenger for the message. You made me suffer for your own feelings for me. We didn't have to have sex. We could have talked, had a meal, seen a film. But even this would make you feel gay, and you felt you had to be straight. You wanted what you considered the English dream: a wife, a fast car, a country house and a London flat. I only interfered.

A couple of years ago I was informed your fiancée had cancelled your engagement. I phoned you to offer my condolences, even though I suspected they might not be welcome. Your reply, though eloquent and generous, was tragic.

'It's true,' you said, 'she called it off last week. But I'm confident she'll come back and that we'll go ahead.

'I appreciate your calling, Paul. You're one of the greatest guys I've ever known. But I do think the next call should come from me, and it should come . . . '

You paused for a moment.

' . . . When I've had my second child.'

There could be no response to that. The meaning was clear. With a wife and two children in place, you would finally be heterosexual enough to be able to have a telephone conversation with me that didn't make you feel homosexual.

'I've been having therapy,' you continued, 'and I've come to realize that I never wanted a man physically, I just wanted love. I missed my parents when they put me in boarding school at an early age and I just wanted some love.'

A dozen years after we split and you still couldn't bear to talk to me. I finally realized how much you love me, though you would deny it into the next world and beyond. It must take a powerful amount of emotion to love somebody so much that even speaking to them makes you feel like you want to do something which is either against your nature or against what you would like your nature to be.

Of course you're not alone in giving the silent treatment to a person who symbolizes your own illicit desires. In my experience, bisexual men as a rule treat their former lovers worse than gay exes do. By denying the person they had sex with they deny the unwanted impulse inside themselves. One such man, upon encountering me at Sainsbury's on a Saturday morning, turned around, ran down the parallel aisle and fled the store. Another, having been with me more than two hundred times over a period of a decade, announced he was completely straight and ignored me for two years before suddenly recommencing relations. You're not the only one, Stephen, you're just the saddest one.

I have to hope that after you've had that second child or maybe the third, or even the first, you'll get in touch. I must pray that you accept whichever it is you need to accept – your history, if you genuinely are heterosexual, in which case you will finally have the maturity to be proud of love given and received in the past, regardless of its form; or your nature, if you're bisexual, in which case you will surrender the insistence that you keep your sexual dance card one hundred per cent heterosexual. It really doesn't matter to me how you wish to express yourself emotionally and sexually for the remainder of your life. But it does seem mighty unsatisfactory that you, the first person I ever lived with, might never again speak to me, the first person with whom you ever lived.

How much do I love you? Part Three: I have your picture in a silver frame. I am looking at it now. You're looking straight at me, ear-to-ear grin, mischievous glint and, oh yes, a glass in your hand. You are happy. Do you remember? You were happy. I remember. We were happy.

I also remember what you told me when we were driving around your university parking lot. I still can't believe you're a bad person. I still can't believe you want to hurt me.

GEORGE

H ow are you these days, fuckwit? Have you seduced
any royalty lately? Have you broken any Tory
politicians' hearts since I last saw your ass? Have
you been given expensive presents which you have
passed on to others? Are you still, goddamn you, drop-dead
gorgeous or has one of the parade of people you plunder
given you the broken nose you were asking for all the time
I knew you?

Which, I have to admit, wasn't that long. We only saw
each other as lovers for two months and as nemeses for a
few more. It's a morbid tribute to you that, like 7 December
1941 (Pearl Harbor Day), you live in infamy years after
you left my life. It's a skill not taught in school to engage
the feelings of someone else when you yourself are not
emotionally involved. I should have felt a *frisson* of fear
when you told me you'd been a psychology major at
university, but how did I know you'd studied the subject to
make people sick, not well?

Even now, if you are reading this, you're probably
marvelling at how worked up I got about you when you
yourself were only giving a polished performance. You
were the one who taught me that the opposite of love is not
hate, it's indifference. I thought that, since I loved you and
you didn't love me, you must hate me. Wrong. You could
care less. I've never been more humiliated. You complete
dickhead, I wish you could feel how I felt the moment I
discovered the person I loved was seeing someone on the
side, and I was the someone on the side.

To think that, when I met you, I thought this was the
quality young man I'd been waiting for, a university
graduate who had come to London from Birmingham with
a business career in his sights. My heart almost leapt for joy

when you told me you were doing work experience for a regional TV company. It wasn't your choice of employer that thrilled me, it was the fact that you wanted a nine-to-five job with the promise of gradual promotion rather than instant success as a pop idol, model or film star, like the witless and hopeless wannabes I so often attracted before I met you. Here was a serious man, an educated man, a voracious reader.

You were also a male escort. It never occurred to me that a university student or graduate could be a gigolo, escort or companion, whatever noun you used to rationalize your behaviour in your own sick mind. I never considered that one of our student leaders at Dartmouth College might have been servicing the studs of the local high school while everyone else was doing their homework. University students didn't do that, I assumed; they had loftier ideals. George, you taught me that some university students do do that, that you don't have to be in the gutter yourself for your mind to be there.

I met you at Bang on a Monday night in 1987. The club had not changed its music policy to the house and garage sounds which had swept the scene since 'Jack Your Body' had gone to number one in Britain that January, and seldom was heard a discouraging word of American rap. Bang had always stayed on the pop side of dance, and the big repeated record the night we met was Rick Astley's future international number one 'Never Gonna Give You Up'. It was certainly not to be our song.

But how was I to know you'd turn me into a bitter and twisted thirtysomething? I'd only popped in to recharge my batteries. Most of the early evening clubgoers were gathered in clusters of twos and threes, but my attention was drawn to a young man sitting alone at a table for four overlooking the dance floor. He looked lost and lonely, although this was probably just a projection of what I wanted him to feel so I could rescue him. I approached him and asked him if he was OK. He replied that he was fine, his name was Tony, he was waiting for his friend from Birmingham, the friend he'd come down to London with to try to make it in the big city. After a short chat I was convinced he didn't need my attention and I didn't crave his, so we parted with pleasantries.

I would be lying if I said I remember what I did for the next hour. I can only speculate that it was my typical evening at Bang, drinking mineral water while most other folk were downing pints of something or other. Perhaps, in the long term, being abstemious has helped my health. It has certainly saved me a fortune. The only time in my life I drank more than one beer was the first time I touched the stuff, at a Thanksgiving evening party at Dartmouth, where an upperclassman who had been trying to get into my pants for months dared me to match him halfpint for half pint. Six halves later he was on the floor and I was completely bored, feeling as if I had consumed several liquid potatoes.

With the exception of the occasional glass of wine with a good meal, I hadn't touched alcohol of any sort since the late 1970s. This enabled me to keep my senses while many around me were losing theirs, although this proved to be a mixed blessing in those few instances, notably when I had jet lag, when I would stay up for the 2 am close of Bang. Certainly I missed the humour of many late-night jokes other people found hilarious. I also never participated in the closing-time pairing off that would take place first inside and then outside the club, when alcoholic consumption blunted the discretion and lowered the standards of lonely hearts. 'U Got the Look' by Prince with the unbilled Sheena Easton was a new hit when you and I first met, George, and I felt that His Purpleness must have observed this late-night ritual at least once. 'Closing time, ugly light, everybody's inspected' perfectly summed up the ceremony. It was like a police line-up where, instead of being accused of past crimes, suspects were vetted for their potential for future lapses.

I am sure I must have danced to a couple of songs that night. Bang knew a good twelve-inch when it found one and was desperate to let it go. A floor-filler was a floor-filler, whether it be hard-core disco or disposable pop. In the seven or so years I patronized the place several records had turntable lives of over twelve months.

But here I go again, George, talking about music instead of you. Can I help it if it's more interesting? But for those few weeks I lost my perspective entirely and took you more seriously than tunes. Can you believe it? You, more important to me than the Supremes? Temptation more vital than the Temptations? I really was mad.

I was in love. I admit it. Have you ever noticed that this process of losing ourselves we call 'falling in love' is literally true? We fall. We come down from the pedestal on which we are perched and we grovel, shamelessly, pathetically, giving someone else the power to make us feel worthwhile. Believe me, you bastard, I learned from you, and I have never again given anyone else that power. I've granted someone else the ability to make me feel happy – anyone does that when they're in love – but I've never again allowed someone else to make me feel worthless just by ignoring me.

So there I was, about to leave Bang after my usual hour's worth of chatting, dancing and downing mineral water, when I see you at the bottom of the staircase with the young man I had talked to at the beginning of the visit. I couldn't believe he – or anyone else! – could have such a friend. You were dressed in a light blue suit with a white shirt and tie, and outclassed the competition by light years. The usual problem of breaking the ice with a stranger spotted across a crowded room didn't apply, since I was already on speaking terms with Tony and could insinuate myself into the conversation naturally. I saw interest light up your eyes and managed to excuse ourselves into a talk for two at a nearby table. If only I had known that interest was not what I naively hoped! I was seeing a potential partner; you were seeing pounds and pence.

You worked me. You presented yourself perfectly – the man with his feet on the ground, the university graduate, the TV trainee. You looked at me with those beautiful eyes, which I later learned were coloured by unnecessary contact lenses, swept aside your medium length black hair, and showed me your deep tan. When we agreed to meet three nights later, on Thursday, I was floating. One of those oddest of moments had occurred, a point in time after which there is no going back. I could not now imagine not knowing you. What had life been like only two hours before? I could not recapture the feeling. Now the world had you in it, and it was a different place.

I've got to be honest, I can't remember what we did the first part of Thursday evening. But I can never forget the second part. It was Good. Forget the second 'o', it was God. I thought I'd gone to Heaven without the usual prerequisite of dying. By surrendering to Nature, we fulfil our nature, and are at one with Her. There are acts of love so sublime we feel there cannot be a happier person in the world. Of course I also felt that way the moment I got the last out pitching my fortieth win of the softball season after two years finishing with thirty-nine, but there were more people present then. You were the only witness to my late-night joy, and you shared it.

So I thought. The following morning, before you left for work, we made an arrangement to see a film another three evenings later, on Sunday night. I was left to contemplate our night together. I became a bit anxious, wondering if I could cope with such a vigorous sex life on a regular basis. At this point you are probably fuming that I could be so presumptuous. I'm blushing at having been so stupid.

You weren't able to make it in from your shared flat in Slough on Sunday night because, as you informed me in your affectionate phone call, trains on the line between Reading and Paddington had been cancelled. But we were able to meet twice that week, and on one occasion we had another rapturous night. You liked to wear T-shirts with U-shaped necks. As a v-neck gown reveals portions of a woman's breasts, these U-necks exposed rounded parts of your own slightly raised tiny tits. They turned me on to an extent I never told you, for fear of letting you know the power you could hold over me.

Unfortunately, your work with the TV company took you far out to East London on Saturday evening, so we were denied a third rendezvous that week, but I was determined not to be disappointed when the last-minute demands of your job kept us apart. After all, the responsibilities of persons in TV are flexible, by the very nature of the business, and your training must not be jeopardized just because I was in love with you and wanted to be with you.

I didn't feel threatened by the demands your work placed on you, because you reciprocated my feelings emotionally and sexually, cooing words of love and satisfying not only my needs but my fantasies. Your voice was so reassuring I wished we could speak every day, but I understood I couldn't phone you because of British Telecom's delay in installing new residential lines. As long as we were together a couple of evenings a week and you were able to stay over one of those nights, I understood the irritating tendency of work to call you away at weekends, once to a TV conference in Manchester, other times to last-minute fill-in assignments in exotic suburban locations. I was so touched when you declared that we had to spend the entire next weekend together, regardless of the vicissitudes of your job, and so disappointed and concerned when you phoned in Friday evening to say you had food poisoning and wouldn't be able to make it.

Still, the pleasures of our week-night meetings overshadowed our weekend disappointments. You gave me a chance to talk seriously about politics and literature, opportunities I did not have in the pop music world. You showed real concern over my slightest problems, such as the night in early autumn you rubbed my hands because you thought they were cold and needed warming. You were so happy to share with me the professional success I was then enjoying. You shared your life story with me to the extent of telling me of all the key figures in your life, including your ex in Birmingham, Nigel, who you assured me was a fine man who had treated you well. You hoped you could one day introduce me to him, a generous gesture I thought indicated a truly open mind.

Six weeks in I was so happy with our relationship I suggested we consider living together. You agreed this was a goal, but thought the timing premature. I respected your feelings, silently reprimanding myself for being overly keen and lecherous. I was nonetheless disappointed that you were not your usual affectionate self as I left you at Paddington that evening. My emptiness at being deprived merely a hug and kiss at the train station made me realize the extent of my emotional commitment to you. I looked forward even more keenly to our weekend together, which had been delayed for various reasons for the full month and a half we'd known each other, and I was delighted when you called late Friday afternoon to say you were on your way over. I prepared an Italian dinner in happy anticipation of your arrival.

That night I ate two dinners. You never showed up and you did not phone to explain. I was beside myself with disappointment and worry. Had something happened to you on the way over to my place? I didn't want to be paranoid and assume you had rejected me. After all, you had called to say you were just leaving work to come over. If you had wished to stand me up, you wouldn't have bothered to ring, you would have just blanked me.

I spent an anguished weekend, arranging to be home as much as possible so I could answer the telephone in the event you called. If I had to go out, I instructed my Nicky, my PA who lived in the downstairs room, to take a full message, including a number at which you could be reached. When I was home, whenever the phone did ring, I instantly hoped it would be you.

It never was. By Sunday night I had to admit defeat. I had spent forty-eight hours examining the crisis from every conceivable angle, and all I was doing was making myself more and more upset. By now there were only two possibilities: something terrible had happened to you or something equally dreadful had happened to your attitude towards our relationship.

Of course there was another option. Your deception had been so skilful and my thinking so wishful I had not considered the obvious. When I went to the Roof Gardens, the Kensington restaurant that transformed itself into a gay club on Sunday evenings, I ran into Tony. I asked him, in evident distress, if he had heard from you or if he knew where you were. Of course, he said, you were where you were every weekend, at home in Birmingham with your boyfriend Nigel.

Birmingham? Home? Every weekend? Boyfriend? Nigel was not your ex, but your current partner?

I detained Tony from the dance floor as long as I thought polite, gently pumping him for information about your flat in the Midlands, trying hard, probably too hard, not to show my shock and desperation. You and Nigel had been a couple for years and shared a place in Birmingham. You went home to Birmingham every weekend, where you carried on your settled social life with the friends you and Nigel had cultivated over the years. Before he left me for the dance floor, your chum said he'd seen less of you now that you were both in London and, if I wanted to know more about your present situation, I should talk to the two girls you shared accommodation with in Slough.

And that was that. That was how, on a Sunday night in October 1987, while hundreds of beautiful well-dressed men around me danced to 'Pump Up the Volume', I was deflated. The love affair I thought was developing into a long-term commitment turned out not even to exist. I felt like a running cartoon character who doesn't notice he's run off a cliff until he sees that his feet are pedalling air. There is the moment of comprehension before he falls, during which he pedals like crazy and grasps for any bit of solid land to break his fall. I was desperate to hang on to any glimmer of hope that I might emerge with some form of continued relationship with you, no matter how reduced.

This was proof that there is death after death. Even after we've been emotionally slain, we reach out for any opportunity to have the killing prolonged, just because we aren't ready to be completely abandoned. When someone has left us unexpectedly, we struggle to get him back just so we can grow strong enough to survive losing him again.

I sat at one of the restaurant tables, sipping mineral water, oblivious to diners in nearby chairs. My moods swung frantically between three feelings. I was outraged at your deception. I was humiliated I'd spent so much time staying in and waiting by the phone when you had no intention of visiting or calling. And I was reaching out for hope, any palliative to ease my pain.

Thoughts of how you had deceived me sped through my mind. I'd spent a weekend commiserating with you for having food poisoning and fever when you weren't ill at all – the only sweating you were doing was in a Midlands disco! There had never been a weekend TV conference in Manchester.

The next morning and several mornings after that Nicky was my father confessor, although there cannot have been a priest in history who heard his penitent recite the same sins so tiresomely. Nicky understood that, when someone is as deeply shocked as I was, repetition is required to make incomprehensible news at first believable and then bearable. I loved and respected Nicky even more deeply for putting up with my psychobabble. Someone lost in love doesn't realize how boring the subject can be to others, though to him it seems the only important topic in the world. There was no other news that October 1987. The stock market crash? The collapse of Communism? Who cared? I loved George and George didn't love me!

One reason I could keep Nicky entertained or bored with regular reports on my emotional state was that this was a story which didn't want to end. Every day or two you surprised me, George, with further evidence of your perfidy. The first aftershock naturally came a few days after my discovery at the Gardens. You hadn't called and, because you had no phone, I couldn't call you. There had been no way I could get you to confirm or deny your friend's description of your life in Birmingham. Consumed with the desire to know the full story, I drove to Slough that Wednesday evening to see you. I knew I was making an uninvited visit, and it occurred to me that a two hour round trip was a long time to drive not knowing if you were going to be in. But I had to see you, and I kept my morbidity engaged by endlessly replaying a cassette of a song I'd written called 'Why Do We Die?'

Surely this was a sight for sore brains: a thirty-eight-year-old man trying to find an address in the side streets of Slough on a dark rainy night with the soundtrack of a song about unexpected impending death. Occasionally I'd get enough perspective on my sorry situation to recall the words of a long-forgotten soul singer: if this is love, I'd rather be lonely.

That night I got to be both, in love and lonely. You weren't home. Your flatmate Sarah, who also worked with you, was, however. To say she was surprised to see me would be an understatement. Although she politely admitted me to your front room and gave me a glass of water, she clearly had no idea that we were lovers. When I told her I'd been upset that I hadn't heard from you since you were to due to visit on Friday evening, she replied, 'Oh, but he was in Birmingham with Nigel, like he is every weekend.'

To Sarah I was some television personality who had just turned up at her front door, and it was testimony to her trustfulness that she didn't keep looking for a hidden camera. I can only imagine how suspicious I would have been if Gene Shalit, the American breakfast television film reviewer, had dropped by unannounced for a discussion of his love life. Sarah was chatty and even started talking about her own romantic difficulties. She was obviously in no position to give me direct information concerning your attitude to our affair, but her complete lack of knowledge about it gave me all the indirect facts I needed. Not only did you go up to Birmingham every weekend, you also sometimes went up for a day in the middle of the week. Nigel had only been down once, but he was a wonderful man who obviously adored you. She enjoyed chatting to him when he rang you because she could sense your love and concern for each other.

No! No! Barf bag, barf bag!

I told Sarah I thought you didn't have a phone. 'There it is,' she said matter-of-factly, pointing to the instrument on the wall, as if it were unthinkable not to have one. She knew you were with Nigel in Birmingham that night because you had called to see if there had been any messages concerning work the following morning. You had a phone after all, you lying bastard, you just didn't give me the number because you didn't want me calling and letting these women know you knew me!

Stunned like a boxer hit by a barrage of blows, I weakly tried to make conversation and enquired what it was like having you for a flatmate. Even in small talk I could not escape punishment. Sarah replied that you were a nice man, and you had lots of laughs about work whenever you did have dinner at home together, but you really were hardly ever there. Without Nigel you were lonely in London, which sounds more elegant than 'sad in Slough', so you went out most evenings and didn't come home some nights. This was especially true since you had met Anton.

Anton? Who the heck was Anton? What were you doing spending the night at his place, and at whose homes had you stayed over before you met him? Resigned to the probability that I was sticking my chin out to Muhammed Ali in the fifteenth round of a title fight, I asked Sarah who Anton was.

'He's the man who's trying to make George famous,' she replied without a note of irony. 'He's the publisher of a fashion magazine who thinks George would make a good model, and some nights after work they have strategy sessions about how they're going to get him jobs in Europe.' *Vulcan* more likely than *Vogue*, I thought ungenerously, as Sarah continued. 'They're going to have their first photo session this Saturday.' George won't have to bring many clothes to that, I suggested in silence. 'Nigel isn't happy about missing a day with George, but he thinks it's worth it if it gets George money and some good trips.'

Bet you George thinks it's worth it if it gets him money and some good trips, too, I mused – but I wondered what the 'it' was. Well, I didn't wonder, I presumed, but Sarah certainly didn't. She obviously believed your story down to the last detail. And why shouldn't she? I had, until I discovered its inherent contradictions, as I would have over time even if I hadn't learned what I did that particular Sunday at the Gardens.

The drive back to London that night was long enough for a couple of rain showers, a few more plays of 'Why Do We Die?' and some serious thinking. When I had first started talking to Sarah, I had thought she'd been kept in the dark and didn't yet realize that you and I were a couple. I had left the flat thinking that I had been hoodwinked and hadn't known that you and I were not a couple. Not only was I not your number one, I wasn't even your number two – there was this stranger named Anton who had pushed me aside with promises of modelling success.

Now, George, I have to tell you, you never had a chance.

I've known lots of male models (no, not that type of knowledge), and they've all been taller than you, almost all
darker than you and nearly all more muscular than you.
Anton apparently thought you could make a good hand or
head model. At some point, I calculated, Anton would
decide you were not going to succeed at modelling and
would stop wasting money on photo sessions. You would
then lose interest in him and might start sleeping with me
again.

This had to be the low point in my romantic self-
esteem. I still wanted you so badly I didn't care if you had
to fail at your career choice and another man had to lose
crate loads of cash for me to get you back. And even then
I would still be your number two – although, I calculated,
if I could have your affections for four days a week in
London and Nigel three in Birmingham, I might turn out
to be the *de facto* number one. Had you reduced me to
this meanness or just brought it out in me – that I could
wish three different people ill so I could have what I
wanted?

My heart leapt for about four seconds the next morning.
That was the time it took for me to answer the phone, for
you to say, 'Paul?', for me to exclaim, 'George!' and for you
to launch into a tirade of abuse.

'How dare you go to Slough last night?' you screamed.

'You disappeared on me, remember? I was worried
there might be something wrong . . . '

'You're the something wrong. Everything else is fine.
Things are good at home and Anton is going to make
me rich. I don't want you ruining things by getting in the
way.'

I had to protest. 'How is going to your flat to see if
you're healthy going to ruin anything?'

For the first time you acknowledged the calculated risk
you were taking. 'I didn't want the girls to know about you
because I didn't want them to mention you on the phone
to Nigel. I don't want to upset him, and I don't want to lose

him. I saw you on weekdays because I was lonely living in London without him. But we're staying together and I don't want anything to jeopardize that.'

I felt I had to point out a historical truth. 'George, you did say you loved me.'

'I did at the time. When I was with you and I was lonely, I loved you. When I was home with Nigel and wasn't lonely, I didn't love you.'

I had to ask the big one. 'What about when you're with Anton?'

'Anton means nothing to me and you know it,' you barked. 'We're just friends. Well, we're not even friends, not like me and you . . . '

'Sarah said you stay over some nights . . . '

'We work late and there's no point going home to Slough.'

'Where does Anton live?'

'He has a flat in Hampstead.'

'That's three miles from me. You could get a cab and be at my place in five minutes. You could stay with me instead of him.'

'Then he would know I see you and he might get angry. Besides, it would be rude after all he's doing for me to leave him just because it's time to go to bed.'

George, I've left a lot of people in my time because it was time to go to bed, and I am unaware any of them had taken offence. But although your logic had as many holes as a Swiss cheese, I couldn't argue with it because more than anything, more even than convincing you I was right, I needed information. In loving you I had been like a doctor attempting complicated surgery with a pocket map of Australia as his guide. It was the wrong type of knowledge and there was not enough of it.

So I went straight to the point. 'Who is Anton anyway?'

'Anton is a very important man, and I don't want you trying to talk to him.'

You proceeded to tell me what big news Anton was – that he was a prince in one of the exiled royal houses of

Europe, that he was a friendly acquaintance of one of the minor members of British royalty, that he was living in London and frequently visiting Paris as the publisher of one of the leading fashion magazines. He personally knew most of the top designers and was going to introduce you to them. You had calculated that you would make at least £85,000 during the next year as a model.

'Is this in addition to or instead of your regular job?' I interrupted your rapture.

'For the moment I can do both,' you replied completely seriously. 'That's why we're doing the photo sessions on weekends, and I can usually get away with not showing up for work one day a week.'

Ahah, I thought, you admit sneaking up to Birmingham in the middle of the week!

'Of course, if the modelling really takes off and I have to do a lot of travelling, I'll ask for a leave of absence. Anyway, I'm going to go now,' you announced suddenly. 'I'm at work. Remember, don't call Sarah. And don't try to call Anton at the magazine. They screen all his calls.'

'What about tomorrow night?' I asked pathetically, desperately trying to hold on to my personal combination of Twiggy and Mata Hari.

'I'm not sure,' you said brusquely. 'Early in the evening Anton is taking me to a reception for a leading cosmetics company. They might want to use me in their print advertising.'

As what? A bar of soap?

'If things go well, we could go on to dinner with their executives. If not, if Anton wants an early night, I'll call you by nine. If I don't speak to you tomorrow night, I'll call you Friday. Bye.'

You hung up. At least, I thought, you had called. That's how desperate I had been to hear your voice. Love really was blind. It had no vision, it possessed no perspective, it knew no self-respect. 'Am I Fool Number One?' Brenda Lee once sang.

Stop the song right there, Brenda. The answer was yes.

I had put my emotional and sexual lives in storage waiting to be with you again. You were so cold to me it turned out I'd put them into the long-term deep freeze. Of course I waited in the following night until nine, hoping against hope you would call and I would see you for the first time in what seemed like centuries. One moment I wished I'd stolen a glance at the telephone in Slough and copied down your number so I could ring you, but I realized that would be useless since you were almost never there and certainly would not be now. It wouldn't be helpful to have either Nigel's or Anton's number since neither of them knew I existed and would hardly welcome a call.

I had to face facts. I was the distant corner of your lovers' rectangle. I had been a fling, a fill-in when you were away from your husband. Now I was a sub-fling, relegated to the sidelines while you played with Anton.

George, that was as low as I got. The bed chamber of our affair had become a chamber of horrors. My love life had become a nullity. I could not now acquiesce in the annihilation of my self-esteem. At 9.01 on that Thursday night I knew you were out doing whatever you had to do to maintain the fantasy you were the next Jean Shrimpton. I faced the fact I would not be seeing you that evening. I decided to make the move that every man or woman who has ever found themselves unexpectedly abandoned by the person they loved recognizes as the first step to recovery. I phoned somebody else.

By the grace of the gods my friend James was home. He was very much in the mood for attending the opening of a club. This was not surprising, considering that as a social butterfly James earned frequent-flyer miles. He wanted to be either a pop idol or a film star and was young enough still to think that, if he hung around at enough late-night parties, he would meet someone who'd give him a big break in show business. Although straight, he didn't mind that the club we were going to was gay: the drinks would be free and we might meet a famous gay pop star. We didn't, but we did meet Paul O'Grady, better known as the drag queen, yea, empress, Lily Savage. I was due to introduce her while co-hosting a Sunday night charity event and was pleased to have the opportunity to have an off-duty private discussion with this icon of the scene. In what were still the early days of AIDS fund-raising, drag artists had done more benefits than anyone, even though they knew their selfless service would not get the public attention that a single perform-ance by a major recording artist would. I admired Paul O'Grady's wit and intelligence as much as I respected Lily's dedicated response to the health crisis.

James liked meeting Paul too. Though not interested in drag, he was open-minded enough to appreciate the achievement of anyone popular enough to help fill a West End theatre. And, though not himself gay, he was open-minded enough to have sex with a man. At least he was that night. For the first time in the two years I'd known him, we made love.

Wherever in the wilderness it was that manna fell from heaven, the Israelites could not have been expecting it. It is difficult to imagine a meteorologist predicting bread showers being taken seriously. I could never have forecast James would prove so affectionate that night and shower me with the emotional sustenance I so desperately needed. Over the two years we'd known each other we'd grown closer and more tactile, but never before had we taken the last big step. I honestly don't know why James gave me his love that night. Maybe it was part pity – he naturally knew the depths of my depression, seeing as I was talking about you to everyone who would listen. Perhaps it was the lateness of the hour. It could have been the free drinks. Whatever it was, it was wonderful.

George, I had no way of knowing what a turning point that night would be. James and I were to make love intermittently for six years. You and I never had sex again.

This didn't end our story, though. Wounds so deep don't heal overnight, and webs so intricate do not unwind. I'd been so obsessed with your part in my life that I hadn't really thought about my part in yours. I couldn't withdraw without helping to sever a few strands.

That Saturday night I went to Heaven. I spent most of my visit upstairs in the Dakota Bar. Why it was called this I'll never know, as it held absolutely no souvenirs of North Dakota, South Dakota or the singer Dakota Staton. The main reason I went there was that the ground floor of the club was dominated by the main dance floor, which at the time pumped out a non-stop sequence of house and garage hits which were not to my liking. Even the Star Bar on the first floor had moved to a high-energy music policy I found tedious. The Dakota Bar, with music by the likes of Whitney Houston and Diana Ross, seemed to be the last refuge of lyrics and melody in the building. Less generous souls might have called it a watering hole for the middle-aged. It was certainly true that professional men in their thirties tended to gravitate to the Dakota Bar.

There I encountered my good friend Dr Charles Farthing. This great man was one of the leading HIV and AIDS experts in Britain. He was, thanks to frequent television appearances, probably one of the three best-known AIDS doctors in the country. One of the most satisfying treats in life is to listen to a friend who knows more than you do about some or many things talk about one of their subjects of expertise. It was always an honour to hear Charles talk about HIV and AIDS because he always managed to be both an extremely caring man and an authority who did not let sentiment colour his science.

On one memorable occasion he allowed me to accompany him on his rounds at St Stephen's Hospital. He informed me that the Turkish man we were about to see was unlikely to survive forty-eight hours. The next day he faced the trauma of a final visit from his family.

'Do I have to see them?' he whimpered.

'Yes,' Charles replied gently, but firmly.

'We never get to stop fighting, do we?' asked the dying man.

'No, we don't,' said Charles.

The doctor held the patient's hand for comfort, but would not insult him by offering false reassurance in words. I was overwhelmed by the dignity of the exchange.

That Saturday night in Heaven, Dr Farthing and I did not discuss medical matters. He asked me how I was and I truthfully replied that I felt awful. I gave him the same old song I had performed for all my friends, telling him in more detail than was probably necessary what had transpired between you and me.

'And the worst thing', I complained bitterly, 'is that I can't get him out of my mind. I think about him about ninety-five per cent of the time.'

Charles became animated. 'I know exactly what you mean. When John left me suddenly, I found I was thinking about him at all the wrong moments, when there was nothing I could have done to help the situation. I realized how out of hand it had become when I was in a staff meeting at the hospital and I found myself thinking about him while we were discussing health matters. When they get in the way like that, they've got to go. Knowing they're taking up space they don't deserve is the first step to breaking the obsession.'

Charles predicted that, as days and then weeks went by, the percentage of time you were on my mind would decline. At first the drop was more of a drip, from near one hundred per cent the first week to ninety-five per cent the second. But those rare moments of relief were like the first rays of sun poking through clouds after a storm. They promised not only that there was the possibility of better weather but also it was on its way. I gradually shed my thoughts of you, my hopes for a future together, my pain at being denied your company. Half a year later I was restored to perspective.

One reason it took so long was that I didn't have either the strength or desire to be rid of you. Anna Ford once told me the best way of getting over a man who had treated you horribly was to do the best you could to convince yourself he was a terrible person worthy not of love but of extreme disdain. Since you were the first to put me through the emotional wringer, and I suppose I was lucky I got to the age of thirty-eight before being taken to the cleaners, I had not yet learned this lesson. I had hopes we would remain friends or potential lovers, or – something.

You encouraged this attitude by phoning me and occasionally seeing me.

You did call me as promised the day after the Thursday evening magazine reception and told me excitedly about meeting important people in the fashion world. The following week you related breathlessly how Anton had flown you from Milan by helicopter to a party where you met a famous Italian fashion designer. You wanted to share with me the thrill of what you perceived as your ascendancy in modelling. You went so far as to speculate that 1988 would be our year, that one night we would be seated together for the première of my as yet unfinished musical, clutching copies of a magazine with you on the cover. It didn't bother you at all that our sex life had ceased. As a matter of fact, for you, it hadn't necessarily stopped – it had just gone on extended hold. Just as Abba never announced their break-up, they just didn't make any more records together, so you never told me we were finished, we just didn't sleep together any more. You knew I would understand that you would be spending your evenings working on the modelling project with Anton, who meant nothing to you personally. Anyway you weren't having sex with him and, if I met him, I would see he wasn't attractive and you weren't tempted.

What you couldn't foresee was that, a few days later, I did meet him. It was Monday night at Bang and, as usual, I was patrolling the terrace with a mineral water. I had assumed you would not be patronizing the clubs now you were spending your spare time with Anton. It didn't occur to me that Anton would want to go to Bang. There you were, a couple, right in front of me. Why did I perceive you as a couple? Because Anton was patting you on the ass, an unlikely gesture to be made by professional colleagues. I would have considered it most odd if a fellow broadcaster of mine, say, Kid Jensen, had fondled my backside in public. His wife would have considered it even stranger. No, buttock-stroking is reserved for persons who have feelings for each other that go beyond the metaphysical.

Do you remember Chief Dan George in the film *Little Big Man*, with his repeated line, 'My heart soars like a hawk'? My heart sank like a stone. Whenever I thought you had run out of ways to shock me, you would always come up with a new one. Anton's gesture told me you and he were intimate, despite your countless denials. There was more evidence, too, later that week when, at his invitation, we went over for coffee after we'd seen a film together.

'I've got the orange juice and vanilla ice-cream you like,' he told you. 'Would you like some?'

The way he offered you your favourite treats told me of the loving pleasure he felt in being able to provide you with what you enjoyed. And, of course, the part of me which was always willing to interpret things to my disadvantage assumed that, since he'd stocked up on orange juice, your favourite breakfast drink, you must often have breakfast with him. It didn't take much prying to discover this was true. Slough was so inconvenient for work in London that you'd moved in with Anton. He was invigorated by your company and the challenge of making you a successful model. Feeling that you should dress the part, he had bought you a new wardrobe, including the item he was most proud of, an expensive black leather jacket.

After a talk about the international fashion press, a discussion I must admit was rather one sided, it was time for me to go to bed. I left you with Anton, his arm draped lovingly around you. I counted my lucky stars I'd begun at least an occasional relationship with James.

The next morning I received one of the most un-expected phone calls of my life.

'Paul, this is Nigel, George's boyfriend. I hope you don't mind my calling, but I got your number out of the address book we keep up here. He told me he was going to a movie with you last night, so I thought you might know where he is. He's not at work. I need to know what train he's coming up on tonight.'

'Oh, hello, Nigel,' I tried to be nonchalant, as if meeting romantic competition was a casual matter. 'No, I don't know where he is. Is he still at Anton's place?'

'What do you mean?' Nigel asked, startled.

'Just that I dropped him off there last night after the movie. If he hasn't gone into work, maybe he's still there.'

This was not what Nigel wanted to hear.

'Do you mean to say he stayed overnight with Anton?'

'Well, you know, he has these planning sessions after work and just stays over.'

'No, I don't know! He tells me he always goes home to Slough.'

'Is he always there when you call at night?' I asked with a combination of mischief and genuine curiosity. How could George pretend to be at a phone number he had left several days ago?

'I just assumed he was there. He always calls me. I get home around the same time every night and he gets in at different times, sometimes late, and it doesn't make sense to waste money on long-distance calls when I'm only going to wind up talking to one of the girls. You mean he isn't at Slough some nights? Is something going on with him and Anton?'

I couldn't believe my desperate conversation with Tony at the Gardens was being duplicated, except your partner Nigel was now in my shoes, pumping me for information. Instant Karma was going to get you.

'I don't know,' I replied honestly.

'Paul, excuse me, but I've got to try to find him. I'll call back some time and we'll arrange to meet up. And here's our number,' which he duly recited. 'George says only nice things about you.'

Huh? I thought. 'Oh, thanks, Nigel, that would be great,' I said. 'I hope you find him. Bye.'

'Bye.'

Nigel's penultimate line echoed in my disbelieving ears. 'George says only nice things about you'? Obviously these were selective things, but I was amazed you mentioned me at all to Nigel. You didn't want me calling Sarah in case she mentioned me to Nigel, but you retained the prerogative to speak to him about me. There was only one conclusion: you wanted to control the flow of information between all the people in your life and told them each what you wanted them to know about the others. What you could never anticipate was those moments when lines got crossed and someone inadvertently blurted out damaging information, as Tony did to me, Sarah did to me, and I did to Nigel.

Boy, did I. Filled with the heady thought that 'George says only nice things about you', I called the Manchester number that very evening at six to see if Nigel had tracked you down. He sure had.

'Paul, I'm afraid I can't talk now,' Nigel began the conversation. 'I'm throwing this whore out of the house. Here, say hello and goodbye,' and he handed the phone to you.

'George . . . ' I started.

'Fuck you,' you interrupted, 'you had to ruin everything. I got home a few minutes ago and Nigel had put all my stuff in the hallway. Can't you learn to keep quiet? Fuck you.'

'George . . . ' I resumed.

'I can't talk now, we're fighting. Fuck you.'

'George . . . ' I stopped when I heard the dead tone.

And then it was my turn to be annoyed. I never did like people hanging up on me, especially if the last thing they said was, 'Fuck you'. I called you back. This time you picked up the phone.

'George . . .'

'It's you again. Fuck off. I never want to speak to you again.' Hang up. Dead tone. Bad move.

In the course of a few hours I had gone from 'George says only nice things about you', to 'I never want to speak to you again'. Except, of course, you did, the next day. You rang me. So much for your self-restraint.

'Why did you tell Nigel about Anton?' you began the inquisition.

'I didn't tell him about Anton. I just said you might be at his place.'

'But Nigel doesn't know I spend the nights at Anton's flat.'

'How am I supposed to know that? You're going to keep your address a secret from your boyfriend?'

'It's easy. I call him every evening so he doesn't have to call me, and Sophie brings any mail that arrives at Slough into work, so I get it the same day. I send him mail from work so it has the office postage frank on it instead of some postmark from Hampstead. It was perfect until you blew it.'

'I blew it? I'm not the one staying with Anton!'

'Nigel would never have known. It took me hours last night to convince him there was nothing going on between me and Anton.'

'You never told me there was,' I jumped at the suggestion.

'There isn't,' you jumped even more quickly. 'You saw how ugly he is.'

'And you thought Nigel wasn't going to find out you were living with Anton?'

'Why should he – until you had to open your big mouth. Haven't you learned what friends are for?'

'What do you mean?'

'Friends are supposed to cover for each other.'

'Even when one of them is lying?'

'Of course. That's especially when they're supposed to cover for each other. If you're my real friend, you should support me in keeping Nigel happy. Otherwise there's no point in our being friends. Do you understand?'

I had to admit that I did.

'So don't ever open your big mouth again, all right? Especially when you're up here.'

'George, I never go to Birmingham.'

'Well, you're invited. After we fought last night, Nigel felt badly that we'd been rude to you, so he suggested we ask you up for a weekend next month. When can you come?'

Incredulous, but unable to resist the invitation, I got my diary and made plans to visit Birmingham two weekends later. During that fortnight you called me twice to fill me in on the luxury hotels you stayed in with Anton when you went over to Paris for meetings with modelling agencies. I knew of them all and recognized you were becoming familiar with the city's top establishments. You gave me strict orders not to mention any of these details to Nigel since you had told him what it was safe for him to know. How you avoided relating any of these adventures to your workmates was beyond me. Talking about helicopter rides in Italy would be far more exciting than discussing what brand of tape to use in a Beta SP camera.

You were the model of good behaviour during my weekend in Birmingham. What you couldn't help, of course, is that I would learn something about you virtually every time you left the room. On one occasion you were taking your daily sun-bed treatment, which explained your perpetual tan, and Nigel was musing aloud about how generous you were to him and how worried he was that you were spending all your money, more than you could sensibly afford, on gifts for him. He pointed out some items in the wardrobe you had bought him, a few of which were pieces that I had given you myself. I even saw the leather jacket Anton had been so proud of giving you. Nigel and you had basically the same measurements, so you wore each other's clothes interchangeably. He had no idea the expensive presents you were giving him had come from other people. They, in turn, had no way of knowing that you were accepting their gifts and then presenting them to Nigel. You would be able to wear the garments later anyway.

Oh well, what were friends for, other than not to tell what they knew? I agreed it was a nice leather jacket and changed the subject to the friends we were going to meet for dinner. You had been thoughtful enough to arrange a meal to introduce me to your Birmingham friends.

We had dinner at a pleasant hotel in the city centre. I was instantly attracted to one of your friends, Mark, and managed to sit next to him at the opposite end of the table from you. In between courses he filled me in on your notorious past. It seemed that London was the latest and greatest port of call in your sequence of career moves. Mark related how the friends assembled had been buzzing about the fight you'd had with Nigel concerning Anton. Nigel had been so annoyed after his conversation with me he had told his confidant, a fiftyish man everyone in your circle trusted. This gentleman had naturally told another of the friends, and the story had gone around Birmingham faster than you could get from London on the train.

'We were waiting for this,' Mark remarked.

'What do you mean?' I asked.

'George is always doing this. Has he taken anything from you?'

'No,' I replied truthfully. 'He's misled me about things, but he's never stolen anything.' I guessed accepting clothes under false pretences did not amount to theft.

'When George was at university he went out with a Tory politician who was a prospective parliamentary candidate. Nigel didn't know about this, of course, not until later. The politician was crazy about George and put him up in a nice flat, much better than student accommodation. He got him a car so they could drive to see each other. When he'd got about as much as he could out of this, George told the guy to get lost.'

At this point I realized it was to my advantage to be out of your love life. Just as I wouldn't think of playing power politics with Machiavelli, I wouldn't wish to battle you in the sex wars. But I also realized something else. You had, from your perspective, let me off easier than anyone you'd ever manipulated before. This doesn't sound like much of an honour and it's not one I put on my curriculum vitae, but in a bizarre kind of way it was touching. You'd never taken anything I hadn't freely given. You certainly hadn't tried to take advantage of me financially. You had even, in your own words in an angry phone call, referred to me as your 'friend'. Sally Field had been right all along: you liked me, you really liked me. It's too bad it wasn't the way I liked you, but at least it was something.

I've never enjoyed cold-turkey endings to relationships, probably because they hurt so much. I've always been one for tapering off, gradually seeing each other less frequently with fewer confidences shared, until it doesn't matter when or whether you see the old flame again. This is how I got over you. One thing which kept me in contact with you through the spring of 1988 was that, having paid my admission, I now had a front-row seat in the show of your love life. As a player, it had seemed tragedy. As a spectator, it was merely farce.

You narrowly got away with Christmas '87. Nigel had been infuriated by several phone calls from Anton, suggesting and then demanding that you spend the holidays with him in some exotic European resort. You managed to convince Nigel that Anton was simply keen to get on with preparing for your modelling project for 1988, but, since not a single photo of you had been published nor one contract signed, this excuse for continued contact with the exiled prince was wearing thin. Your partner demanded that you spend more spare time with him in Birmingham. You skilfully managed to fob Anton off with some stories about family get-togethers that required your presence.

On one occasion in the New Year Nigel rang me disconsolate, seeking reassurance. Why did you spend so much time with Anton? He was convinced you weren't sleeping with him now, but thought you probably had at the beginning, despite your denials.

'I guess it was just like with me,' I answered off the top of my head. 'He wanted to get him interested and, once he did, stopped.'

'Do you mean he slept with you?' Nigel froze.

I had no idea he hadn't known. 'You said a couple of months ago that George had told you he was seeing me,' I remembered our first conversation.

'See, yes. Sleep with, no. What a bastard!' he exclaimed. 'Not you, Paul,' he modified, 'George. How often did he stay with you?'

'About once a week for a month and a half,' I calculated. 'I'm embarrassed to say I thought it was a big deal, but I had no idea at the time that you two lived together. He told me you were his ex, a wonderful man I would love to meet one day.'

'He always says nice things about the people he's sleeping with, even while denying he's sleeping with them. He's such a slut – nothing personal about you. When was the last time you slept with him?'

'October,' I replied, immediately sensing how much lighter my emotional load had become after the passage of a few months.

'I'll have to confront him about that,' Nigel said intently.

'Just don't put his things in the hallway first,' I suggested.

Nigel actually laughed.

'And don't worry,' I added, admiring his determination to stand by his wayward man despite all indiscretions. Was this true love or masochism? 'George has always spoken of you as his lifelong partner – at least, ever since I found out you were living together.'

'Let's hope Anton has found out,' Nigel closed the conversation.

Anton hadn't found out. In March I got an out-of-the-blue call from the prince himself. Was this my first telephone conversation with royalty? Did exiled royalty count? Years later King Constantine of Greece called at my house, looking for my lodger, who had serviced his car, but that wasn't half as exciting as what Anton had to say.

'Paul, excuse me, this is Anton calling,' he opened politely. 'Have you seen George this morning?'

'No, I haven't. Why should I?'

'Because he's supposed to be here with me and he isn't. He told me he was visiting you this morning at TV-am.'

'That's impossible, Anton, because I don't bring people from my personal life to the studio. I haven't even heard from him lately.'

'This is so annoying,' said the peeved prince. 'He really is on the verge of blowing this completely. I've set up a very important meeting with the editor of a top fashion magazine. These people will not be kept waiting, and if you don't come to an appointment you've made, they don't want to see you again. George doesn't realize the extent to which I've put my own reputation on the line for him.'

Neither did Anton, but he would soon find out.

'Have you tried Birmingham?' I asked.

'Why would he be there?' Anton answered with another question, as surprised as if I'd suggested you were on the moon.

'He might be home with Nigel,' I speculated.

'What do you mean?' The conversation was turning into a quiz.

'You know, he sometimes takes a mid-week day off to be with Nigel.'

'Do you mean to say he is still sleeping with that nobody?'

'You can call him a nobody, but he is his lover.'

'What do you mean? I'm his lover!'

The wheel of hurt had turned again.

'I'm probably not the person you should be talking to about this, Anton,' I tried to be discreet, even though I was secretly loving it.

'Who else can I talk to who knows him? Those cheap friends of his? Paul, I respect you, you're a man of achievement, this Nigel is a nobody. Why does George insist on anchoring himself to a loser when I give him the best opportunity he'll ever have?'

'Are you his lover?' I asked naively, but desperate to know.

'Of course. You know he moved in here. We have sex regularly. I fuck him all the time and it's fantastic.'

I bet.

'I take him to Paris, I put him up in all the best hotels, I introduce him to the leading people in the field. Who else is going to give him this treatment?'

'Nobody else, that's for sure,' I answered his rhetorical question.

'Paul, you don't know what I've done for him. I gave up the woman I was thinking of marrying. She would have become a princess. I have treated George as if he were a princess.'

Don't put him in the will, I felt like screaming.

'I've introduced him to friends. Do you know how important that is, for me to present him to important people as my partner? What am I going to do now? Does he love this Nigel or does he just see him for crude sex?'

'I think he loves him, Anton, and I think you should know that. Logic doesn't play a big part in something like this.'

'In that case I'm going to have to cancel his contracts before they are signed. The fool! He would have made at least £85,000 a year. Where else is he going to get such money?'

'Not in his present job,' I sympathized.

'I'm going to have to have his name removed from all

papers of co-ownership. I'm going to have to pack his things and put them in the hall.'

That wouldn't be a first.

'I'm going to have to change the locks. I'm thinking of changing my job anyway. I've had a good offer with a company based in Dallas.'

Good, I thought, they love royalty there and wouldn't have a clue whether you are in exile or not.

'But, Paul, what am I going to do about my feelings? I love him.'

At that moment I felt terribly sorry for Anton. You had snared him. This was not just a paw-in-the-fox-trap job. You had him by the heart.

'I did, too, Anton, before I found out the truth.'

'You mean he used to have sex with you?' he gasped incredulously.

'Oh, yes. Ever hear the Kinks song, 'Who'll Be the Next in Line'?'

'He never told me that! He said you were good friends who went out to movies together.'

'And how did he tell you we became friends? Did I hang out at his office looking for cinema companions?' I couldn't help getting sarcastic after hearing such a tame and concise summary of our relationship. 'I don't know how you put up with it,' I said honestly.

'Because I love him. The way he gives himself to me is so complete, I feel I have to be understanding. He says he'll grow out of this phase and soon we'll be together, just the two of us, every night, but I can't help wondering what he's up to when he stays out. And now this Nigel, this loser in Birmingham. Who would be in Birmingham if he was somebody in the world?'

Simon Rattle? I didn't wish to interrupt.

'How can I give up the person I've been looking for all my life, the person I really love? It's inconvenient he's a man, but I've accepted that. But if he was a woman, we'd say he was behaving like a slut!'

'You're not the only person to use that word to describe George,' I pointed out.

'Who else has? Who else knows that about him?'

'Nigel.'

'Nigel? Does he know about me? Some nobody up north knows that George is making a fool of me?'

'Anton, I can assure you that Nigel does not know you and George are lovers. He thinks he stays at your place for convenience. He'll be furious when he finds out what's been going on between you, if he ever finds out.'

'He's going to find out right now! I'm going to call them and straighten this out! First I'll cancel the meeting with the editor, then I'll take care of George. He'll learn what it's like to play with me. I'll talk to you soon about this, Paul. I hope we can be friends. You're a man of honour.'

'Why, thank you, Anton,' I verbally blushed, hardly expecting a compliment in such an insult-filled conversation. 'I look forward to hearing from you.'

And hear from him I did. And Nigel. And you.

The next call came from Nigel, twenty minutes later.

'He's done it again! That whore! I wondered why he was getting so soft inside his ass!'

'I gather you just heard from Anton,' I said nonchalantly. 'He spoke to me a few minutes ago.'

'Yes, I heard from Anton. Who does that ponce think he is? Who the fuck cares who he is? Where's George?' he rattled off the questions like shells from a machine-gun.

'He's not with you? I thought he was with you.'

'I thought he might be with you.'

'Anton thought he was with me.'

'Who is he with?'

'Maybe he's with nobody. Maybe he's on a train.'

'Going where?' Nigel seemed to be changing roles from irate cuckold to keen detective.

'Birmingham to London?' I guessed.

'No. He hasn't been here.'

'London to Birmingham?'

'No. He isn't due here.'

'Maybe he's at work,' I suddenly grew practical. 'We're all forgetting that it's a work day, and he should be at work. Have you tried him there?'

Nigel did, and you were there. How you managed to have an explosive conversation with him while pretending to everyone around you that you were talking about work must have been another tribute to your skills of persuasion. As for myself, I was so pleased to be out of your love life now I couldn't believe it. Chicken, rooster and fox all seemed to be running around with their heads cut off at the same time.

The next call was from you.

'What is that bastard Anton doing calling you about me?' you roared.

'How did he get my number?' I asked in return. 'I never gave it to him.'

'Neither did I. I never wanted you to talk to him. What a sneak,' you howled, 'he must have peaked into my diary.'

'I don't like people I haven't given my number to calling me at home,' I pushed it, relishing one of the rare moments I had scored a point over you.

'I'll tell him not to do it again. And don't speak to him if he calls. He's going to want to check every story now.'

'Have you spoken to him today or did you just talk to Nigel?'

'I talked to Nigel and then told Anton what I thought of him calling you. I told Nigel that Anton wanted to possess me, but he couldn't have me because I already had a partner I loved. I told him it would only be a few months, I'll be famous, I won't need Anton any more, and Nigel and I will be rich, so just hang on.'

'Did he believe you?' I wondered if you could visualize my jaw hitting the floor.

'He seemed to. We worked out a compromise I'm happy with, that instead of me coming up to Birmingham every weekend, Nigel comes down here sometimes and stays with me at Anton's place to make sure everything is platonic.'

'Did Anton go for that? He sounded pretty mad to me.'

'Anton just wants a fuck every few days to keep him happy. It doesn't bother me, he's awful in bed, it just keeps him thrilled that he's making his little protégé famous, which is what I want anyway.'

'He hasn't cancelled your contract?'

'I convinced him not to tear it up yet, to keep it and have it signed in a month if he's satisfied with the way things are going.'

'So you've really calmed him down?' I marvelled.

'He just wants me to reassure him. That's easy with him. He's so busy being busy he only has a little time to deal with his personal life, and if he has the impression it's going OK, that's all he cares about. Anyway, I better call Nigel again. If Anton tries to talk to you, tell him you haven't spoken to me.'

Your new arrangement sounded good, provided all parties agreed, but they didn't. Anton entertained Nigel for one weekend and found the experience unbearable. I know because he told me. Sorry, George, but once he had the number, how could I keep him from using it?

'Can you imagine their audacity?' Anton protested. 'Can you imagine how I felt, having to sleep in my bed while someone else is screwing my boyfriend in the next room!'

I admitted I would find this arrangement difficult.

'So it's come to a head. I've got to be in Europe for a few days next week. Because it's Easter, George has it in his head that Nigel is going to come down for a long weekend and stay in my house while I'm away. He is not! I'm not having Nigel having sex with George in my house while I'm not there!'

'It's bad enough while you are there,' I tried to inject a little morbid humour. Anton trampled over my contribution to the conversation and went directly to his next point.

'So I'm having someone from a security service protect the house. Obviously I don't use it very often because I don't want people interfering with my privacy, but in this case I will not hesitate. If Nigel shows up and tries to enter the house, he will be arrested.'

Was he serious? George, I'm asking you – I have no idea. Even if he was a real prince – and how do I know he wasn't making that up – could he get protection whenever he wanted? Could he, a foreigner, try and prevent a British citizen entering his flat as a guest of his domestic partner? Would you, with your back to the wall, rise to the occasion?

We'll never know what you would have been capable of in this situation because you had already gone one step too far. It was a baby step that on its own would merely qualify as a prank, but in context it was the very last thing Anton could bear.

Before he had to go away, a couple of days before Easter, Anton called me from Paris.

'Paul, I can't believe it, but it's true! It's over, I'm changing the locks.'

'What can't you believe?'

'Listen to this! I tell you this because you are, as I have said, a man of honour and you can appreciate how horrible this is. Last week I took George to Paris for a day.' Anton named a hotel I recognized as the *crème de la crème* of international innkeeping. 'The following morning it was time to check out. George told me to go to the cashier to settle the bill and he'd be down shortly, he just had to finish packing. I told him he shouldn't have been so lazy and went downstairs without him. Time was of the essence, we had a plane to catch.

'Two days later, back in London, I received a letter from the concierge. "It was a pleasure to see you, as always, Your Highness, but there is one point that puzzles me. I am wondering why you did not see fit to settle your minibar bill upon departure." I called him, spoke to him, and figured out what happened. George had cleared out the minibar and taken the liquor to Birmingham to give to Nigel as a souvenir of his trip to Paris!

'Can you believe it? My family reputation called into question because George insists on presents for Nigel! Well, if he insists on settling into the sludge of Birmingham, he can wallow in it. I hope he's happy living his low life there! Actually, I don't, Paul, I don't hope he's happy, but I can't even afford to think about him any more. He never wears the leather jacket I gave him either and whenever I ask him where it is, he says it's up in Birmingham. He must have given it to Nigel. Anyway, I have some family business to attend to. My assistant is taking all George's things out of the flat and arranging for them to be picked up so I'll never have to see him again. He and Nigel deserve each other.'

And you know, George, in a funny way, you did. I was convinced, right then and there, that you and Nigel were indeed meant for each other, and that it would be wrong for you to be with me or Anton or the King of Siam. That you ruined your chance to have tens of thousands of pounds spent on developing you career just so you could rifle a minibar for Nigel says more about your love for him than any simple words could do. Time and time again in this horrible half year you had affirmed your love for him in ways that were individually laughable, like giving him a sweatshirt I had bought for you. Added together, they showed that you lived your life for the idea of the two of you as a couple. You spread yourself around to give the two of you a higher standard of living. And he loved you so much that he let you do it, time and time again, knowing that no matter how intense or demeaning your latest affair, you would always return, even while the affair was still in progress, to him.

When Anton threw you out of Hampstead, you and Nigel called to see if I'd let you stay in my guest room until you could find a new place to live. Nigel came down and helped you move in and, about a month later, to move out. He approved when I took you away for the week we had always promised we'd share in Rome. Although this was a major freebie for you, I felt I had to keep a word I'd given even months before and under different circum-stances. And, like our now mutual friend Mark from Birmingham pointed out, you did not take advantage of me beyond accepting what I offered. It was a civil and pleasant week.

It was our last. We never made the transition to good friends. Shortly after you moved into your new flat, you were fired by your company. With no job in London you left the capital. Anton felt this some sort of righteous judgment. He called me once later that spring to fill me in on how you and he had finished.

'We'd booked a holiday for late April some time previously,' he told me. 'Of course I informed him after the minibar business that he wouldn't be coming with me on holiday. Do you know, he begged me to take him? He told me I could shag him silly, his words, no questions asked, no commitment, I could shag him silly if I just took him on holiday. He knew, of course, it would be a first-class vacation, and he didn't care how he lowered himself to get it. Well he didn't get it! I don't talk to him any more. I do want to stay in touch with you, though, Paul, and I'll invite you to dinner soon.'

A year later I ran into Anton in an airport departure lounge. 'Paul, how are you?' he greeted me with a smile. 'Recovered from our mutual friend?'

I told him that time really does heal all wounds.

'And wounds all heels,' he said. 'I'm told things have been difficult for him ever since. But he had his chance for a better life, with both of us, and he blew it. I'm seeing a good woman now and I hope to start a family. I don't stay in England much now, but I do hope to invite you to dinner one day, as I said.'

I haven't been asked to his place yet. Where is his place

now? How did the fall of Communism affect his family's place in Europe? Do you know? Do you care?

I doubt it. You have a strangely admirable way of moving on without regrets. We only spoke a couple of times on the phone in 1989 and 1990. Once we went out to dinner and, after you assured me everything was going well with Nigel, I dropped you off at the Fulham flat of a man you were staying with in London. I didn't want even to begin to try to wrap my brain around what that was about.

Two years later we ran into each other at the London Palladium at a performance of *Joseph and his Amazing Technicolor Dreamcoat*. You were wearing one of your amazing u-neck t-shirts. You still hadn't lost your looks. I felt silent sympathy for the man you were with. There you were, with your choirboy face, your smooth tan flesh and your seductively curvaceous chest.

You know, for a moment, just a moment, I forgot everything that had passed between us, and I was meeting you again for the first time. I wondered for a second if we could ever be something together. I wanted to reach out with my hands, stroke your little breasts . . .

And tear them off.

TERRY

You died yesterday. I hope it was peaceful. Rebecca told me it was, and Tony thought so too. You passed away at night, three minutes after I woke up and noticed the time on the digital clock. To quote a favourite old song title, you even woke me up to say goodbye.

Which is better than I could manage. To paraphrase another song, you said goodbye, I said hello. After knowing and loving you for a dozen years, my last words to you were, 'Hi, Terry.' But, under the circumstances, I can't think of anything else I could have said.

I had called you the weekend before to see how you were doing and spoke to an extremely upset Pierre. It was obvious from his description of the two operations you'd endured that week that you had entered the final phase of your illness. It was also apparent he had entered the stage all caring partners go through, but cannot envisage until they are in it: he was suddenly facing being alive without the person to whom he had dedicated his life. He saw more darkness than light.

Caring for a sick partner can be open ended both emotionally and physically. The rest of the world doesn't just take second place, it retires to the sidelines. When the loved one departs, the person left behind is not only lonely from loss, he has to cope with the emptiness of having no one else of near equal intimacy left.

Pierre had instructed me that, when you were going to sleep, you customarily turned off your mobile phone. Recently, however, you nodded off so often the phone was frequently still on and one of your visitors would answer. In the final days you were in such a state someone would pick up the phone for you even if you were awake.

You were alert when I rang Tuesday night. The person

answering handed me over to you. After an exchange of greetings, you said three words I never wanted to hear.

'I'm dying, Paul,' you said, your voice frailer than I had ever heard it. The tone was shaky, but the meaning was unmistakable. After several years of talking about HIV and keeping track of your T-cell count, after two and a half years of going in and out of hospital, and having nearly every AIDS-related illness I had ever heard of, you had neared the end. You were too weak that evening to receive further visitors, but you might be able to handle a visit in twenty-four hours. I should arrange it with Pierre. You signed off simply but sweetly: 'I love you, darling.'

I wondered whether I should come see you or not. Of course I wanted to, but it was obvious that you had a variety of friends and family in constant attendance. At least some family are going to be present at a final vigil; in your case it was quite a few. A person's lover is going to be there; for you it was not only your current lover but your ex, the great love of your life. There were also two men who represented the range of your friendships, one a sober pal of your own age and the other a wild older man.

Where did I fit in with this crowd? I didn't, and that freed me to come and see you. I couldn't be expected to be either a member of your family or a lover, so there was no embarrassment in not being either. I was a man who had known you longer than any of those outside your family and better than any of those inside your family with the exception of your mother. Even if we were not going to be able to have a final conversation, I had to honour the unique part we had wound up playing in each other's lives.

None of these considerations prepared me for the sight that greeted me when I walked into the ward just before 7.30 that Thursday evening. There was no deathbed vigil because there was no bed. You had been wheeled into the day ward, hooked up to your IV, and were surrounded by a crowd that had assembled for one time only, to be with you when you died.

My first thought was: *Guernica*. This is an emotional *Guernica*. I don't remember the exact circumstances under which I first saw Picasso's depiction of the bombed Spanish city, but the work had left a deep impression. The painting conveyed to me both the intensity of suffering and its unique personal nature. This was what presented itself to me now.

Deathbed scenes are always difficult. There are bound to be conflicting emotions. I recall one vigil with an heroic mother who, having recently suffered the sudden loss of a daughter, was now enduring the gradual death of a son. There was another family member present who, having refused to accept the sexuality of the man who was dying, was desperately trying to make amends at the last moment for fear of having lost his love for all time. At this same gathering, there was one person in the room who had previously tried to kill the patient and at least one other who had abused him. Having won his forgiveness, they were now present as if nothing untoward had occurred. At least two people present were HIV-positive themselves, glimpsing an unwanted preview of their own possible future. All were wearing their worries on their faces.

I couldn't refer to this of course, nor to *Guernica*. It wouldn't be polite to say, 'You guys remind me of a famous air raid'. So I walked over between you and Rob, who was clearly in control of the proceedings, said, 'Hi, Terry', kissed you on the cheek and added that I'd brought some chocolate for people to have, at which point I laid out several squares bearing the imprint of the Chocolate Society. I usually brought you chocolate when I visited you in hospital because you had a special appreciation for the quality stuff I loved: truffles from Clarke's, blocks from La Maison de Chocolat and so forth. 'Paul has always been a connoisseur of chocolate,' you informed your family. That was the last thing you ever said to me.

Rob interrupted without missing a beat. 'Tony's in the kitchen,' he said. 'He'd like to talk to you.'

This was a class brush-off. Maybe because I'd known you guys for ever or perhaps because the circumstances were so drastic I couldn't avoid picking up on what was happening, but it was obvious that I had to be gotten out of the room for your sake as quickly as possible. It wasn't that it was me, it was just that I was a person, period. The entire scene had become more than you or anyone at the end of their life could possibly be expected to endure. You had become, like Billy Pilgrim in his Tralfamadorian zoo, the main attraction in a place you didn't want to be, under circumstances you would have given anything to change. I had seen your beautiful eyes hundreds of times, but the look in them this night was new. They spoke of incomprehension, near panic and being out of control of the situation.

And there was something else I had once seen long ago in one of the most unbearable moments of my childhood. My father ran over our dog Danny with us in the car. We all piled out, parents preparing to take him to the vet and children in various stages of hysteria. Danny looked straight at me, straight into me. His eyes said then and for ever: why do I have to die now? What did I do to deserve death? I don't want to die, not yet, not this way!

I never thought I would see that look again, but I saw it in your eyes that night. During the year you worked for me we had discussed death and what might come afterwards, but that had been theoretical. This was real. Dying is not like imagining dying. In your eyes that night in St Mary's I saw that you knew you were on the brink, that, although you might have prepared to leave this life, no one could ever really be ready to take the leap into the unknown.

Twelve years had passed since we first met in Heaven in 1983. You were one of the attractive teenagers working in the club. Your eyes commanded my attention. They did not just interface your internal and external world – they lured those on the outside to come inside, to sort out turmoil and contradiction, to satisfy need. This was not an invitation, it was a summons. Those of us who fell under your spell could not resist. Circe and her sirens had to make music to attract the attention of sailors. You only had to look at them.

Because you were always open and forthcoming with me, it surprised me that you were very shy, almost un-communicative, with people you didn't know. This is the secret that people on the same emotional wavelength share. They are as open with each other as they are with themselves because, for some funny reason, they are a part of each other. One person fills a gap or satisfies a need in another, the same happens in reverse, and you have two people who not only have no problem finding things to talk about but also can't shut up. Based on the high number of times we spoke for very long periods of time, I can confidently say that, allowing for sleep, toilet and meal breaks, we could have talked for ever.

This presupposes we never met anyone else with whom we could talk for ever. You did. You met Rob. Not only did you become part of each other, you were each other. For the eight years you were together you were referred to by all our mutual friends as 'Rob and Terry'. (For some reason that pleases the ear, the shorter name of a duo almost always comes first; in my profession 'Rice and Lloyd Webber', 'John and Taupin' and 'Lennon and McCartney' are famous examples. It is not a slight on Lloyd Webber, Taupin, McCartney . . . or Terry.) The needs you two fulfilled in each other were giant versions of desires mere mortals possess in baby size. Knowing and loving you two allowed me to see emotions played out in Technicolor, Cinema-scope and Sensurround. I often feel that I have run the emotional gamut from A to Z, but when I consider what I've seen you two go through, I realize you had an additional twenty-six letters of experience. I never saw such complete union as when you were happy together; I never witnessed such desolation as when you temporarily split up and could not cope apart. You were Dependence and Devotion and

Devastation with capital Ds, and you made me feel I have lived my life in the lower case.

I want to write this now, while you are still alive in my mind and my heart, before these feelings turn to memories – and they will. We say that we will never forget somebody, that as long as we live they live on inside us. That is true to an extent, but only to an extent. For years after he was killed in a car crash in France I dreamt annually of my schoolmate Steve. He wasn't doing anything in particular in my dreams, he was just there, present, looking at me from across the classroom. His image was still in my mind; the sensation I felt was that I was seeing the real Steve. But it was Steve as he had been one, then two, then ten years before, frozen in time more precisely than the mythic Walt Disney on ice. It wasn't Steve as he currently would be in the spirit world, heaven, reincarnated or dematerialized. His image, though accurate in a visual sense, gradually lost its impression of life, because nothing survived of personality or movement, or of impressions previously gathered through sensory stimuli.

If in life you had come from behind and put your hands over my eyes and asked me to guess your identity, I would have been able to tell it was you because of the feel of your fingers. I would have known it was you because I touched your fingers often over the course of a dozen years and certainly every day you worked for me. Often, during long conversations about your health, your love crises or the origins of your hang-ups, we would make a sandwich of our hands. I could have identified you by touch even without my other senses. And I could identify you from the way you hugged me, tightly, with all your (as we both must have known) diminishing strength, long embraces that neither of us seemed to want to end. As long as you were embracing someone you were alive, emotionally and physically. No person or illness could interfere.

And Terry, darling Terry, this will go. Maybe I could identify you by touch if, thirty years from now, you did return and put your hands over my eyes, but I'm afraid this is mighty moot. What will gradually leave me is the every-day memory of how your fingers felt, how tightly you squeezed me in a hug, how sweetly your lips touched mine when we said goodbye every evening. The next phase is that I will merely remember I knew how your fingers felt, that we embraced in a characteristic and meaningful way, and that we kissed as a symbol of friendship. Later, after a few years, even some of these memories will go. You will be reduced to impression and anecdote.

I know this because it has happened to me already with people from my life. For example, all I remember about the deaths of two classmates is a funny story in which their drowning sets up the punchline. I remember their deaths more than I do their lives. I have no wish to be disrespectful, as I have the vague sensation that they were perfectly friendly girls, but what I love them for is that they gave me this memory.

Their names were Susan Becker and Karen Berg, and they were in my sixth-grade home-room at Greens Farms School. Mr Whitmire was our teacher. One day the girls went into Long Island Sound in a small craft and were swept into deep water, where they drowned. This was sad, but children seem to take death less drastically than adults. Whether this is because they have less idea what is being lost or because they have the perspective to know it doesn't amount to a very high hill of beans is a matter I will leave to psychologists. Suffice it to say that, by the following week, when Mr Whitmire fell ill and we had a substitute teacher taking the class, we were all pretty cool about it.

The substitute, a young woman apparently in the early days of her teacher training, began the morning by calling the roll.

'John Allen?' she asked matter-of-factly.

'Here,' answered John.

'Susan Becker?' she continued.

There was a two-second pause.

'She's dead.' The anonymous voice came from the back of the room.

Shock filled the face of the tyro teacher. She had been asked to take a class with a deceased pupil on the roll and nobody had warned her!

'Karen Berg?' she went on, trying to make we impressionable children think that this revelation of mortality hadn't shaken her.

No two-second gap this time.

'She's dead too.'

The teacher stopped roll-call then and there.

'We don't have to do this today,' she said, placing the class book down on her desk and getting on with the first lesson.

I tell this story whenever anyone asks me about the effect of death on children. As kids we were nonchalant about the sudden passing of our peers. 'She's dead too!' As adults the episode seems a ghoulish combination of horror and hilarity. Everyone I tell it to laughs. The underlying premise of the tale – that there could be a class where two-thirds of the first three students on the roll died without warning – is unacceptable considering our expectations about the lifespan of children and the knowledge of the grief of parents who have lost daughters. I express my condolences to Susan's and Karen's folks now, should they still be with us.

Yet that is my sum memory of two human beings I once shared a classroom with every day. It's a forty-five-year-old man's memory of something that happened thirty-six years ago. The lives of two perfectly fine people have been distilled into one anecdote, and it's an anecdote in which they're already dead.

I don't want this to happen to you, Terry. I want to live to be ninety, but I don't want to get there and remember that I loved you, but forget how it felt to love you. You were the most intensely alive person I've ever known. You must not be reduced to a passionless history.

And so I write now, without any emotional censorship or any care for how overly dramatic I may seem to those who never knew us. I describe my feelings for Terry now so that, upon re-reading them in years to come, I have a better chance of re-experiencing them.

I'm glad to know that I don't have a problem which has plagued my mother ever since the death of her own mother. My grandmother, a marvellous no-nonsense non-judgmental woman who would rather get on with things than worry about them, seemed invincible to emotional problems until the sudden death of her husband who, sitting at his desk one day, asked, 'Where would I be without you?' and slumped over dead.

It was, on paper, a fine way to go, getting the unpleasantness over with quickly and giving the survivor a memory of having been loved and appreciated. In real life Gram, as we called her, didn't see it that way. She entered an emotional tailspin from which she never recovered. Within a few years her health suffered. She experienced increasing memory loss and grew afraid to be alone. She died from cancer.

My mother found that the intense awfulness of those final days was such that she could not think of Gram without those memories coming to the fore. Cruelly they blocked her recollection of the happy, mature woman she had known earlier and for years kept her from enjoying thoughts of her beloved parent.

I'm glad to say this didn't happen to me with my grandmother. Within a year she would occasionally appear in dreams, and she would do so in her prime. This won't happen with you either, Terry. Yes, I know I will be haunted by the severe circumstances of our final phone conversation and our last meeting. I will never forget the look in your eyes that seemed to have a glimpse of the imminent and didn't want anything to do with it. But, just as in my life you have been the definitive Person With AIDS, living each stage of the illness with the extreme drama and intensity that characterized your life, so you have been the model Beautiful Young Gay Boy, frightened but faithful friend, preposterous hellraiser and dedicated assistant. I can't imagine anyone playing any of these roles with finer definition than you. You weren't just alive, you were Life, not poured into a bottle, but trapped inside a body. Those of us who loved you couldn't help but give you room and be grateful we weren't bouncing off life's walls like you were.

Your death has hit me harder than any previous losses, and this includes my best friend from college and even a short-term ex. One reason is that I suddenly feel I must be middle-aged. This is not to say that I feel a particular age or that I feel old. It's just that, if I knew you from when you were seventeen to when you were twenty-nine, I knew you for your entire adulthood. If I did, and you are gone and I'm still here, then I must have lived for some time. There never was much time to waste. Now there is none.

My very survival suggests that, no matter how close I feel to you, there is a part of you I never touched. As I consider the men at your hospital vigil and those attending your funeral, I realize that several of them will follow you soon. Together you shared the late-night life I never knew – and, occasionally, the days-long binges I never conceived. The drinking, the drug-taking, the anonymous shagging just never interested me. It's like smoking. I've never done it, but I can't take any credit for beating it because I've never had the temptation to smoke. Sticking a tobacco stick in your mouth makes about as much sense to me as putting a carrot stick up your nose. Each is a plant, either is an orifice, and it doesn't seem to matter which is which.

But you did it all. My early nights and your so-late-nights-they-were-early-mornings effectively put us into different time zones. The satisfaction you derived from getting out of your tree or having sex on a side street with a stranger is unknown to me, most likely because I don't feel motivated to do these things. I love music, I don't want it to become part of the paraphernalia of drug-taking. I like sex, but with someone I know, at home.

I hope you didn't feel this difference in leisure habits kept us from being as close as we might have been. Indeed, you would probably have considered an unlikely and unappealing sight a Paul stripped to the waist, sweat pouring from all pores, a drugged-out disco daddy blowing his whistle at four in the morning. My disinclination to play this role has probably kept me alive while loved ones around me have died. Can it be that the cost has been to stay a half-step removed from my dearest friends? I love you guys so much, you'd think I would always want to be with you, and yet I didn't join Kenny at the Coleherne or you at the L.A. or Ashford at the East End leather bar. I hope this doesn't mean that going to bed at eleven or twelve kept us from being even better friends.

I don't think so, and not because I'm complimenting myself. It's just that you're the type of guy who had many aspects to his personality. Different individuals satisfied your various needs. You had people in your life who were utterly incompatible with each other, yet you loved them each ferociously and they loved you devotedly in return. I do not claim a special place in your heart in competition with your other friends; I merely claim one place. Others occupy other spots. Some of these spots are larger in size, but that doesn't matter. You loved us all, partly from need, partly from appetite, and partly from the goodness of your gigantic gay heart.

In the 1970s some friends of mine who knew I was acquainted with both Elton John and Paul McCartney asked me to compare the two. I would always reply that, when people who knew Paul met, they talked about him for about fifteen seconds and then got on with their own lives. This was because, his historic talent and achievements aside, McCartney occupied a space in the same world we inhabited and lived by our rules.

On the other hand, when people who knew Elton met,

they couldn't stop talking about him. He did not live by our rules; he did not live our life. Elton was an enigma. There was no single person who knew every aspect of him. This was not because he held back from his several passionate relationships, it's just that his needs required disparate individuals to play different parts in his life.

It has been one of the great satisfactions of my adult-hood to see Elton achieve integration and fulfilment in his personal life. But it is his younger self which reminds me of you. I'm going to dinner tonight with Rob and Tony. I know it won't be long before you are brought into the conversation. I also know that, once there, you will not leave it for a long, long time. We will, I'm sure, try to make some sense of you and we will, I'm equally sure, fail. No matter how many dear ones we have in no matter how many years each of us live, there will never be another Terry.

You were on a one-man crusade to prove that the Chaos Theory applied to human behaviour. You could be in one mode of personality and a few moments later be unrecognizable in your actions. The most extreme example was the 1993 Pride Weekend.

The previous month Rob had left you, you had split up, you had decided to live apart – whichever description makes you guys more comfortable, it had happened. He was, you said, determined to make it in the music business and felt that your constant demands were a drain on his energy. Although he was only going a few miles away and no other man was involved, you reacted badly. You were devastated, and we spent many long conversations trying to give you confidence that you could make it on your own. In low moments you would reaffirm that Rob was the love of your life, no one could ever replace him and it was pointless trying. You faced the imminent end of your life without the man who gave it meaning, so you might as well give up there and then.

A casual observer might conclude either that you had it

coming for being so difficult to live with or that Rob was a heartless beast for leaving you as you approached your gravest health crisis. A person dealing with the emotional fall-out day by day, in contrast, had neither time nor need to judge either of you. Considering you angel, devil, victim or catalyst was of no use in helping you deal with your moods.

After a month I'd honestly thought you had defeated the demons. You affirmed on a daily basis that you had proved you could live without Rob. After weeks of worrying whether you could get by without him, you announced that you had adjusted. You were going to be good friends – you spoke regularly on the phone – but you didn't need to live with him.

Then came Pride. At the end of work on Friday afternoon I gave you a pep talk that I hope wasn't too pretentious or condescending, but was probably both. I told you that, since you had been successful in coping with the changed circumstances, you didn't need to escape from reality over the weekend. There was no need for one of your days-long binges. You agreed and promised to sleep over at my place on Sunday night to avoid the temptation to keep partying. This way you would be ready for work on Monday morning. We kissed, I wished you a good Pride and watched you walk down the path to the gate.

It was the last I saw of you for a while. You encountered Rosco at Pride and you were away. As I discovered weeks later when my American Express statement came through, you abused my credit card in a way I would not have conceived possible – you went to a Chinese restaurant in the East End and spent over £300. That's some Peking Duck. Perhaps it was because, as one of our friends suggested, Rosco likes his champagne. Maybe you got a cash advance for other purposes. It could be you took a measurable percentage of Pridegoers for a Chinese buffet. Whatever happened, it was a gross and knowing betrayal of my trust.

This wasn't the first time you had misapplied my money. One Christmas I had given you £300 to buy photography equipment. You had showed me samples of your work, and I realized that you possessed genuine talent. Only lack of funds was holding you back from becoming a formidable photographer. I gave you a £300 cheque with a playful proviso that, during the next year, you shoot a photo session with me. I never liked posing for publicity pictures, and I thought it would at least be bearable if we could do one together. I also wanted to give you the feeling of participating in a trade-off, that giving such a Christmas present wasn't treating you like a charity case.

An entire year went by with no photo session. As a matter of fact, an entire year went by with no Terry. I didn't hear from you at all. Another twelve months expired without word. Messages on your answerphone were not returned.

Finally, I had to get in touch. I was informed by a mutual friend that you had been diagnosed HIV positive. There was no time for delay. Whatever form our friendship was going to take, it was going to have to do so now. I invited you and Rob over for dinner with another guest, and you came.

I made two important discoveries in the aftermath of that meal. One was the reason you hadn't been in touch since I gave you the Christmas cheque. Instead of spending the money on photographic equipment, you had used it for personal purposes. So this was why we had had no photo session! There was no photo equipment!

You were afraid to take forward steps in any occupation. Indeed, at this point, you had quite simply become afraid. This was the second after-dinner discovery. The young man who had become a star of the scene had taken such a knock to his self-esteem that he hardly left the flat. It was Rob who came to your rescue, almost bullying you into undertaking a photo shoot with one of his acts, providing a safety net by reminding you the snaps wouldn't be used or even widely seen if they weren't to your standards. In that spirit Rob called me. Having heard me say at dinner that I needed a new PA, he wondered if I could offer you the job. I was delighted to, and you accepted.

You may have been pleased, but you were also petrified. Nervousness can precede any new engagement. You were so scared you took an overdose the night before you were due to begin at my house. You spent the day in hospital instead.

Tuesday you made it over and by the end of the week you had calmed down. You felt secure in the job, and you were good. I can recall with dread the shortcomings of some of the people who have worked for me. There was the body beautiful who rated films by the number of times the leading muscle man took his shirt off and who preferred Americans to English men because more of them had undergone cosmetic surgery. I sadly recall the previously dear friend who took a self-assertiveness course when he discovered his HIV infection and started asserting himself with me, requesting a seventy per cent pay rise and claiming I was exploiting him by not paying him advance royalties on a book that hadn't yet been published. I remember the self-styled aristocrat who smugly commented on the leadership challenge to succeed Margaret Thatcher: 'Isn't it funny? I have a personal connection to each of them except John Major. My father knew Heseltine and Hurd went to my school.'

I remember all my PAs from failed to flawless, and I had no complaint with your year of work. Well, one. Sometimes you missed a day or arrived in the afternoon because you had overdone it the night before. I forgave these lapses because I saw them as occasional setbacks in the longer campaign to alter your body clock from late nights to days.

It worked, for a while. I was thrilled as you grew in confidence and self-respect. You drew a genuine feeling of achievement from your work and were proud when you knew you had helped me. Often I was touched by your concern for my personal and professional well-being. Rob was thankful, too, certain that the elevation of your moods and reduction of stress had added at least a year to your life. There could be no more wonderful result to our efforts.

This all stopped with Pride '93. By the time I discovered the credit-card outrage, I had something more serious to worry about. Your binge had not stopped at the oriental eatery in Mile End Road. You had embarked on one of your trademark drink-and-drugs weekends. I knew, sadly, I would not be seeing you on the Monday morning when you failed to turn up at my place as pledged on Sunday night. Typically in cases where you were breaking your word, you did not phone either to apologize or to explain. I learned the real story from a concerned third party, who told me on Tuesday that, still without sleep, you had returned to Rosco's on Monday night and, in the early morning hours, taken a blade and slashed your arm like a violinist bowing his fiddle. You were in hospital after a serious loss of blood.

I went to visit and you were curiously subdued. Subsequently I realized this was not because you were particularly bothered that you had hurt yourself. As a veteran of several overdoses, it was only the form of self-injury that was different this time. No, you were quiet because, having come down from your binge, you were aware you had misused my credit card and were terrified of my response when I made the discovery. You couldn't even be sure I didn't know already.

Here was a logical inconsistency typical of our Terry! You had just done yourself far greater damage than I could ever inflict on you, but self-destruction was second nature to you by now. Paul losing his temper – now there was something to fear! Perhaps dreading my reaction when I eventually discovered the credit-card abuse, you pre-empted my worst option by announcing you were quitting as my PA. It wasn't personal. You were never going to work again. You knew you were dying and you were going to have fun in the time that remained. Tony could take your place as my PA, various government benefits would take care of your financial needs and Rob would pitch in whenever something was urgent.

Another Terryesque contradiction! You were quite happy to slash yourself because life was meaningless without Rob, but you were sure that, whenever things got tough, Rob would be there. Over time I saw Rob grow tired at being manipulated by the emotional blackmail of your drastic cries for help. You do not show your love for someone by threatening to kill yourself if they don't do what you want.

And threatening to kill yourself you did again, within the week, and this time you almost pulled it off. As had happened before, you refused to be confined in hospital and signed yourself out. A friend was deputized to keep watch over you to make sure you didn't repeat your Nigel Kennedy-with-knives routine, but of course no one can keep another person in his sights twenty-four hours a day. Your guardian angel had to go to the local shop and left you unattended for a few moments. He returned to find the door locked with no reply to his increasingly frantic knocking. He got the police, who forced the door open and found you on the floor, lying in a lake of your own blood. You had slashed your other arm and added a gash across your stomach. Had you not been rescued, you would have died.

It is said that suicide is the ultimate selfish act. There is no consideration for those left behind, whether it be family members facing a lifetime of grief or thousands of commuters late for work because a person goes under a train. You were brutal in your disregard for the feelings of others. You would show Rob for not loving you enough – you'd make him feel responsible for your suffering and, if you succeeded in killing yourself, you'd have him feel guilty for ever! The rest of us, who did not approach Rob in importance, were irrelevant. What was the friend who went to the shop supposed to do with the trauma that would inevitably have followed his discovery of your bloody body? I am sure this question never occurred to you. You were consumed by your anger, furious you had been deprived of the thing you wanted most, the thing which made all the other things you were furious about bearable – Rob's unquestioning and all-accepting love. You were so mad you were willing to make us all miserable. Our unhappiness was trivial compared to the magnitude and importance of your distress. You knew we were miserable when you hurt yourself because you saw our reactions whenever you were in hospital, but consideration of our feelings was not going to be a factor in stopping you from the summer re-runs of 'Terry's done it again'.

And nobody was going to restrain you when you got it in mind to go out drinking and meet men. Even you couldn't stop yourself. Often you apologized for showing up late for work, sometimes an entire day late, by saying that you'd only gone out at 11 pm for one drink, but that had led to a second, and by then you'd met someone and . . .

You even did it when we went abroad. During the year you worked for me, I invited you to accompany me on three-day trips to Paris and Hamburg. I wanted to give you the gift of travel while you were still healthy enough to leave England, but I loved your company so much this was no hardship for me. Hardship never, inconvenience sometimes. You took arrival in a new city to be a licence to experience all its nocturnal pleasures. Although Paris and Hamburg are both only one hour ahead of London, you entered a completely different time zone. I would go to bed around 11 pm, which was your cue to begin the revels.

One night in Paris you asked me to go into the Marais with you to share the first drink, so you could grow comfortable with the surroundings of the bar. Sober, you were the shy Terry and did not want to be either alone or hassled by the attention of unwanted strangers. Once you had downed your first drink and felt at home, you sweetly kissed me goodnight and wished me pleasant dreams. You were moving into gear and, by your subsequent account, overdrive, visiting the toilets, cruising the Tuileries at 4.30 am and spending the early morning hours with a waiter.

I had hoped we would walk that morning to Sacré Coeur, an uphill but pleasant walk of a couple of miles from our hotel near the Madeleine. I awoke prematurely around 5 am, and was disturbed to discover you hadn't returned. There were so many possible explanations for your absence it wasn't worth dwelling on any particular one. I fought off my insecurities and went back to sleep, only to wake up at 5.30, and 6, then 6.30, beginning to realize that it wasn't a case of your coming back that night, but when you would return the next day. I then woke up every ten minutes and at 7 decided to forget about sleeping and get up. I figured that, wherever you were, churchgoing was not on your mind.

I enjoyed my usual Parisian breakfast of *jus d'orange* and *petit pain au chocolat*, and hiked up the hills to Montmartre. Since I usually go for weekends in Paris three times a year and always walk around except when it's raining, I've actually gotten to know the city about as well as my home town of New York. Even so, I passed a couple of churches and squares I hadn't previously encountered, and this added to the pleasure of a sunny summer morning.

When I neared Sacré Coeur, I felt a pressing need to go to the toilet. It was still too early in the morning for bars or restaurants with facilities to have opened, so I was left to the mechanical mercies of my first Eurotoilet. A confirmed technophobe, I had never attempted to use the eyesore in Soho Square, the first such glorified outhouse in London. This architectural intrusion in a classic square survived the 1987 hurricane while two giant hundreds-year-old trees fell on either side.

Now across the Channel, I had no choice. Getting in was easy. Getting out was another matter. My French may have extended to *jus d'orange* and *petit pain au chocolat*, but it did not cover equivalent phrases for 'step on this button' or 'push this lever sideways so you can get out'.

I stared panic in the face. You were not with me. I had no idea where you were. I could not rely on your assistance to free me from the prison of the Eurotoilet. And what if you had returned to the hotel and had started to worry about me? The cubicle had no telephone, so I could not call you to reassure you I was OK. It was still early in the morning and the tourists had yet to swarm Montmartre. If I shouted and banged against the walls of the toilet, I would not likely be heard and would merely develop a sore throat to go along with my injured pride. I longed for the old female toilet attendant who, in the days before mechanical conveniences, stood guard at Parisian comfort stations with the expectation of a gratuity.

All these thoughts raced through my mind in the course of about fifteen seconds. I saw a handle and knew it was my only hope. Step right up, Paul, one chance and one chance only for the Escape from Eurotoilet! This was the big one: I would spend the next hour either admiring the splendour of the magnificent church or contemplating the banality of the water closet. Almost like a disembodied spirit watching surgeons bring life back to a body on the operating table, I observed myself surrendering to fate and pulling the mystery handle.

Sunlight streamed into the toilet. I was free. I felt more relief leaving that toilet than I had experienced inside it.

I triumphantly walked the few hundred yards to Sacré Coeur, feeling I had triumphed over all the obstacles modern man had put in my path. Never did self-importance turn to humility so quickly, for the minute I was inside that marvellous monument to faith I was put in my place.

The people who built this house of worship forced themselves for years to overcome every challenge until they had achieved their only acceptable result, the successful completion of the project. This is a type of self-discipline the modern workplace rarely demands or even offers. You don't have to be religious to be in awe of individuals who devoted themselves to a single project for a measurable percentage of their lives.

Now, of course, you'll probably tell me the whole thing was pre-fab and built by slaves. In our cynical age we have to be prepared to surrender almost any noble thought. But, as I stood under the great dome of Sacré Coeur that day in 1993, I didn't feel even a scintilla of cynicism. I was in a sacred place, theological considerations aside. The noblest thoughts and deeds of humans who had lived and died before me had made it sacred.

In that sublime moment I had a pure thought. I would light a candle and dedicate it to your health. This was not to say I believed that, if you lit a candle and left a donation, your prayer would be answered. God does not need lunch money, and the whole notion of bilking the distraught of their spare change seems a pretty sick scam. But this was the first time I had been in Sacré Coeur since I was a student in 1970, and I had the sudden quaint notion that perhaps, if I lit a candle and left the church while it was still burning, it would glow until I returned another twenty-three years hence. Perhaps the subject of my thoughts would be as alive as the flame for those twenty-three years too.

Don't worry about my sanity, Terry, even in that momentary surrender to romance I did not believe that leaving a room with a lit candle inside was a cure for AIDS. But candles have become a symbol of our struggle, as we attend every year the candlelit vigil in Trafalgar Square in memory of lost loved ones, and it seemed a beautiful variation to light a candle in celebration of a precious one still living. I knew, if I could return to this beautiful spot after twenty-three years, that I could and would do so after another twenty-three. Why couldn't you be in Paris with me then too?

I exited by the front door and paused for a moment to

survey the cinematic view of Paris that Montmartre provides. I then descended the steps which begin the trek back to the city centre, my heart light with the feeling that I had somehow managed to come up with what was, at least for this morning, a sane solution to an insane question. I arrived at the hotel, expecting either to find you asleep or not to find you at all.

I was not prepared to find you very awake and with a Frenchman. He was a waiter, you later told me, but he had certainly not waited with you. While I was at Sacré Coeur, you had returned to the room and had sex, on my side of the double bed, no less. Of course you'd been safe, you'd come on his face.

Well, what should I have expected? I might go to another town for restaurants, churches and museums. You ate of the flesh, worshipped at its temple and enjoyed its exhibits. When we were abroad, you were only occasionally the Terry who had sober days with me back home. You were more often the fun-loving boy who, once strapped into his seat for the night, was off on a roller-coaster of thrills.

With only a sigh of disappointment, for all your friends knew the futility of trying to resist your *alter ego*, I went off for lunch, a walk and a museum. You would sleep most of the afternoon and join me for dinner. The evening meal, it turned out, was the time of the day our holiday itineraries most often intersected. I was concluding my day's activities; you were beginning yours.

The waiter really liked you, by the way. Almost all your anonymous conquests did. He even called you a couple of times at my place in London, trying to arrange more meetings. But by then you were back home with Rob, with no interest in reviving a mere holiday fling.

So it was when we were in Hamburg. The logistics were a bit more challenging there, since we were staying at a friend's place on the outskirts of town, but you discovered that he and his girlfriend lived at the end of a subway line.

You could cheerfully disappear late in the evening shortly before I went to bed, guaranteed a full night's adventures before the trains started running again in the morning.

On one occasion we arranged to meet for lunch the next day in the middle of town. You had managed to get a few hours of sleep this time, at the home of a Hamburg lifeguard you had picked up. He was the second person you had been with that night. The first didn't count, since he was a nameless figure in a lightless room – leave it to you to find a dark room in a strange town. The lifeguard was a hunk you had met in a bar and fancied sufficiently to go back with. Although his occupation required him to save lives, he was not overly interested in saving his own. He did not ask you to use a condom while fucking him, and it was only your good will that led you to use protection.

A lifeguard who doesn't practise safe sex! Is it any wonder some of us despair? You did your bit to make sure you did not transmit HIV, but some of the people you encountered made zero effort not to receive it. We could go into a deep psychological discussion here. Perhaps some of these individuals are already infected and have given up the fight. Maybe some of them still think they are young and invulnerable. It could be some find the risk exciting, like Japanese diners downing potentially poisonous fish. The difference, of course, is the fish-eaters know within the hour whether they're dead or not. No fish is so tasty it's worth months of uncertainty or years of suffering.

I'm not preaching to you of all people. We spoke about this several times. Unlike David, my New York friend who probably contracted HIV before anyone knew it existed, you had unsafe sex after the original health warnings. You did so in one of your lowest periods, when you had experienced what was to be a brief split in your relationship, and were so depressed you didn't care what the medium-term future brought, even death. Years later, on occasions when you made what seemed like your eight millionth visit to the hospital, you would say, 'Paul, I would give anything for my health.' Somehow we have got to find a way of convincing despondent young people that they will one day be happier and they must not do anything at their low ebb which might doom them later.

One characteristic of your self-indulgent spells was that you would always be extremely apologetic about them after the rush of drink, drugs and sex had worn off. When we got home from Paris, you deeply regretted you had not spent more time with me, that you had subjected me to possible embarrassment by bringing a stranger into the hotel where I, not you, was the registered guest, and that your sexual activity had been on my side of the bed. This was your super-ego talking. Sober, shy Terry knew the behaviour of tearaway Terry was unacceptable. I have never known a Dr Jekyll who kept apologizing for Mr Hyde as persistently and as sincerely as you. Freud would have tied you to the couch until he had made an exhaustive study of the war between your deeply felt conscience and your utterly irresponsible id.

Why did we put up with it? Almost every other person behaving the same way would have been deleted from the diary a long time ago. But put up with it 'we' did, and that plural is important. I wasn't the only person who loved you despite your preposterous behaviour. Everyone did. You disappointed us when you damaged yourself, of course, and we were mad that we were being manipulated again. But we all knew that you were genuinely not in control and, although we longed for you to be strong, there were times when you gave in to your inner demons. You were the angriest person I've ever known, not in everyday behaviour – you were incredibly meek – but in the un-resolved fury that may have been a result of your first few years. You told me often of your feelings about your illegitimacy and how you wanted to meet your biological father one day. You spoke often of being touched inappro-priately by two older girls when you were a toddler. You were furious this had happened, and that it had left you with an unanswerable question. Was this unwanted interference what had made you gay or would you have preferred a man anyway?

As I've said, your loss bothers me more than any AIDS death to date. In addition to making me terribly sad, it reminds me of my own limitations. I couldn't be closer to you than I was, though I would have liked to, because there was only so much Terry to go around, and there were other people in your life. Partly because you compartmentalized your life, I became close with only two of your friends, only got to meet a couple of others, couldn't stand one, and never met your family until the final hours.

Most importantly in terms of my own failure, I could not make you successful in your career just by wishing it and offering a helping hand. This might seem a trivial consideration. No true friend holds his chum's professional success a condition of his affection. But that isn't the point.

Sustaining a media career for a quarter of a century is like running a twenty-five-year-long obstacle course on a highwire. There are plenty of traps and it's a long way down. The best way for me to cope with my continued public life is to pretend that it's easier than it is – failure is unlikely and success is the probable outcome of any endeavour. That way I reduce professional stress. A corollary of this is that success should be within the grasp of all my friends. It isn't healthy for me to think I'm a statistical freak. If I have enjoyed a rewarding career so far, my chums should be able to do so too. Otherwise I have to face the fact that success in any endeavour is uncertain and my own future is not guaranteed.

I could not make you a success. I could not launch you in your chosen career of photography, nor could I entice you to stay in my employ. You died without realizing your potential. This doesn't diminish my love for you, and I'm sure it rarely crosses the minds of others who cherish you. But it gnaws at me. I don't want to die until I've sucked dry every ounce of creativity within me, until every project

I want to do has been completed. I don't want to think I might go before this has been accomplished. My inability to help you succeed lets me know that I might. Furthermore, I have no certainty of a positive outcome to any project. Every one of us in public life is alone with our particular success without guarantee it will survive tomorrow.

You never fully developed your mind. You were the brightest non-professional person I ever met. That is a compliment, dear, not an insult. When in a sober one-on-one moment, away from the scene and the crowd, you would startle me by your citation of musical and artistic figures usually appreciated only by the *cognoscenti*. When you began receiving regular treatment for HIV and then AIDS, you showed the encyclopaedic knowledge of pharmacology that typifies PWAS. You were also capable of expressing in sensitive moments observations on the human condition that humbled me in their insight. It was a great wish of mine that this wonderful mind, guided by this big and beautiful heart, could have been used for uplift and reward. It will remain a disappointment to me that both were too often kept busy dealing with overpowering emotions. There was more going on inside you than within any friend I ever had.

Maybe that's it, darling. If I am a statistically unlikely individual, at least I know one when I see one. You knew one too. Even though we were each one of a kind, together we were two of two kinds. We were, in the seconds when we embraced, not alone.

I can't believe how much I miss you.

CHRIS

This letter is a bit of a cheat. All the letters I've written in this book so far have been to people I literally never see for the various reasons you never see people – you lose touch, you break up, they die before you. You're different. I 'never' see you in the figurative sense. You're very much still alive and we do talk occasionally, but I 'never' see you – we see each other a couple of times a year whereas we used to see each other every day. The reason we 'never' see each other is, basically, that you've found your own life and you no longer need to be with me on a regular basis. We are happy without each other. This is the best reason for 'never' seeing someone I can think of.

Of course I remember our first meeting. How could I forget it? Your Welsh acquaintance – I wonder if you even remember his name now? – approached me in Heaven and asked if I would listen to a tape of his friend's group. This was defilement of sanctuary! All Radio 1 disc jockeys received unsolicited cassettes in the post, John Peel by the bagload, but these were sent to the network address. Sometimes one of us would be stopped in the street and handed a tape – as a matter of fact a man once gave me his demo cassette on the Metropolitan line at Baker Street station and briefly became my lover – but this, too, was at least in public.

Heaven, on the other hand, was my retreat, my hour-and-a-half Friday or Saturday night battery recharge with the boys. Often after a DJ job or a trip abroad I would just drop in to 'get the vibe', to be in a room full of gay men, to be at peace with my pals. Here was a place where we were always treated as private persons. Like death and taxes, sexuality is a great equalizer.

I had realized this when I made a pilgrimage to the Bitter End in Greenwich Village to see Ann Peebles sing 'I Can't Stand the Rain' and found myself in an audience of only ten people, one of whom was the legendary musician Al Kooper. Two others were a middle-aged white man and a teenage black boy wrapped around each other, making tongue examinations of the interiors of each other's mouths that did not appear to be of a dental nature. This was the first time my college boy self had seen same-sex passion across age, racial and economic divides. I quickly learned that these gaps simply do not exist for gay people. As a matter of fact differences make people more attractive. Who needs to go to bed with someone like yourself when you already are one?

So here I was in the foyer at Heaven, luxuriating in the presence of a thousand happy homosexuals and free of the pressure to perform, when Mr Gay Wales 1982 comes up to me and asks if I would listen to his friend's demo. Sacrilege! Nonetheless I had not yet mastered the art of being subtly rude, and I said I would do so.

Every person in the profession who receives cassettes in bulk knows that over ninety-five per cent of them are awful. This is what you and I would call 'a living tragedy'. At any given moment there are thousands of would-be pop stars spending all their money on tape reproduction and postage costs, living on the headiness that hope provides. Most of them will ultimately not achieve their goals. By that time they will have become interested in other pursuits, so that, far from being bitter about their inability to become international superstars, they will consider the struggle a worthwhile experience in itself and will happily leave it behind.

When a DJ or A & R man or manager puts on a tape and hears what he knows will be a hit, he feels like declaring a national holiday, the experience is so rare. But I had this experience when I slotted the Kajagoogoo demo into the tape player of my little Fiat outside my flat one morning in

October 1982. I hadn't even put the car into gear when I myself was floored. After only ten seconds – before you had even begun to sing, I have to admit – I knew I was hearing a hit. I checked the track listing. 'Ooh to Be Ah' it was called. Not much guidance there! But the vocal then began with its lyric about 'glossy mags' and the other trappings of popular culture and I got a second burst of adrenalin. Just like Chuck Berry writing in the early days of rock 'n' roll, this song was talking the language of teenagers. I listened to the other three songs on the tape, but they could have been recitations of the day's stock market prices, they were so unnecessary for my conclusion. I had actually received a tape from a group who were going to be successful! I had actually been handed a top ten hit in Heaven!

Then came the spooky part. I checked the source of the package so I could get in touch with you to share my enthusiasm. Out of a nation of possible addresses, you lived down the street! Fate was bringing us together, although for what purpose I hadn't a clue. I phoned you and we arranged a meeting at your flat. When I came over, you kept me waiting for a quarter of an hour. You were applying your make-up!

This reminded me of the international discothèque queen Regine, who kept producer John Boundy and I waiting at her New York club while she got her hair done for a radio interview. You made sure your image was complete before you met me, even though we were just going to have a personal conversation. There could be no clearer indication that I was meeting not Chris Hamill, but your creation Limahl, the name being an anagram of your surname.

It does happen occasionally that you believe in someone when there is no real reason to do so. I recall when Billy Idol left Generation X. There were about three people left in the world who believed he would make a career for himself. One was his girlfriend, another was his friend Mark, who made T-shirts, and I was the third. I recall buying Billy a few vegetarian meals – a member of the Clash had convinced him that, when a person eats meat, he or she internalizes the pain and anger of the animal at the moment of its slaughter, so he stopped feeding on flesh completely. During these meals Billy would treat me to his career plans, most of which simply revolved around being famous. This sounded like a road map to the interior of his own head, yet I had a gut feeling he would get there. The image was great, a pretty boy with an attitude and an Elvis sneer, and it was just looking for someone to plug it into record production and promotion. Billy went to live in New York and found that someone, the manager of a star group with spare money to spend on launching an artist in America. The rest is, if not history, at least several successful years in Billy's career.

And, looking at you with that ridiculous hair-do and make-up, I believed. With the exception of a rare genius like Stevie Wonder or Prince, who deserve all the rewards they get, popular success is a function of three factors – sufficient talent, hard work and fortunate circumstances. You had sufficient talent, you were putting in the hard work, now all you needed were the fortunate circumstances. In vigorously promoting yourself, to the extent that you would field a friend with a demo tape in a gay disco, you were virtually providing your own fortunate circumstances. You invited me to the next rehearsal of Kajagoogoo two days later in a Fulham garage.

A garage! I had nightmare visions of being bombarded with sound in a small space and brought plenty of cotton wool to stuff in my ears. Because of a freak accident in gym class in junior high school, in which I suffered a partly perforated left eardrum, I was always sensitive to bass and drums in my left ear. I remember returning home from the Reading Festival one night in the mid-1970s. My ear was still ringing the next day. From then on, I always brought cotton wool. I could not care less if someone near me at a concert thought it amusing that someone who made his living out of music should take efforts to turn down the volume of music. I was determined not to suffer permanent hearing loss, the fate of several rock stars.

I reported as scheduled to the Fulham garage and took my place in front of the band. I could almost have been a second lead singer I was so close. We've all heard reference to 'garage bands', young people forced to play in their family garages because they had no access to other facilities, yet rarely thought of how small garages are. On that occasion I could almost have reached over and adjusted Nick Beggs's hair-do, a blond dreadlock creation that resembled Bob Marley's hair on a drug more serious than his trademark marijuana.

The cotton wool insulated me from pain. Even if it hadn't, a form of elation would have made me ignore the throbbing in my ear. I heard another would-be hit. After the short session, we all huddled together like a football team. I told the group I was particularly impressed by 'Shy Shy', and made a couple of structural suggestions I thought might make it even more commercial.

You invited me to the band's next gig, a support date at The Venue in Victoria. I have many fond memories of this club. Tina Turner on a comeback appearance with her dancers at the time of 'Let's Stay Together', reeling in disbelief with Sting at the audacious Splodgenessabounds as we judged a *Melody Maker* best band contest, ushering a thrilled Jimmy Cliff to meet an equally excited Jimmy Pursey of Sham 69. But my best recollection has to be of you dedicating the first public performance of 'Shy Shy' to me. I was later deeply touched when the sleeve of the single carried the line: 'Special thanks to PG'.

By this time the band had decided to change the name of the song to 'Too Shy', hoping to avoid accusations of imitating Duran Duran and Talk Talk with another double-barrelled expression. Kaja already had the 'googoo' at the end of the group name anyway. The Duran sensitivity was particularly understandable since that group's Nick

Rhodes was co-producing the single of 'Too Shy' with Colin Thurston.

I had first met Nick at Legends. Then the most fashionable nightclub amongst young and trendy pop stars, Legends was run by owner Campbell Palmer. This extraordinarily big-hearted man treated the place as his front room, entertaining show-business favourites with great generosity. On one occasion the disc jockey Mike Read announced with regret that he would no longer be able to come to the club at night. He was going to be presenting the Radio 1 breakfast show and would have to return to his Surrey home early in the evening.

'That's no problem,' Campbell enthused. 'I'll give you a flat.'

I'll never forget the expression of amazement that came over Mike's face upon hearing this offer, but, to his credit, he graciously declined. On another occasion I was seated with Campbell and pointed out to him that Siouxsie, leader of the Banshees, was in the restaurant and might appreciate some champagne. When it was brought to her, the waiter explained to her that it had come from the man at that table over there, pointing in our direction. Siouxsie later came over to thank me, assuming I had been her benefactor, and was subsequently always very sweet to me.

There was one time when Campbell's enthusiasm led him to utter a terrible gaffe, one I'm sure he wouldn't mind my sharing with you. I was in the club with Peter Straker, the singer and actor who was a great friend of Freddie Mercury, another regular Legends patron. Straker was in fine form, and Campbell was highly amused by his wit.

'Oh, Peter,' he bubbled, 'you should be a star just like Freddie!'

As with Mike Read, the initial facial reaction was unforgettable. One thing you don't do is remind a performer that he is not famous. But Peter forgave Campbell this unintentional indiscretion and saw the humour in the situation. We were all grateful for a club where we could eat, drink and dance in friendly company. Most nightlife centres around getting out of it and screaming to make yourself heard. This incarnation of Legends remains in memory for its combination of pleasure and civility.

As such it was the perfect venue for Gary Numan's post-concert party. I was introduced to two boys down from Birmingham, Nick Rhodes and John Taylor. They enthused that I must come to see their band's first London gig the following evening at The Venue. They were so full of excitement and hope that I could not decline. Indeed, I was genuinely touched by their dedication and felt, if they could put so much of their hearts into their group, the least I could do was show up for a performance.

I went to The Venue next night with no expectations and was genuinely impressed. I thought this group would be successful, providing they got another lead singer! For on that night Simon LeBon was audibly nervous. Subsequently, of course, I came to appreciate his charisma and, more importantly from my perspective, his contribution to Duran's recordings. But that first time, he was just another edgy out-of-town kid trying to get through his debut in the Big Smoke.

As I had promised Nick and John, I went backstage after the show and offered my critique. I was intrigued that the band huddled around, with the exception of Andy Taylor, who stood back. This body language proved to represent the dynamics within the group: Andy was the first to leave it.

Chris, as I relive this post-concert scene, I'm very moved. I'm in touch with something elemental in our business, a youthful combination of a desire to achieve, a willingness to work and, above all, a hope so strong it becomes belief that great success is not only possible but will also be achieved. As four members of Duran Duran listen to my every word, not only for encouragement but also for any suggestion that might improve their act, I am receiving the energy of four young men who hope and believe with all their hearts. What comes after this moment must take a different form from what is presently envisioned, for the possibilities open to the extremely successful artist cannot be imagined until success itself is achieved, but this moment of purity, of people expressing their essential selves, is one to cherish. It could be with any band of young hopefuls. It just happens to be with one who will fulfil their dreams.

And you know how Duran dreamed. You remember how Nick said upon co-producing 'Too Shy' it was his intention that within two years Duran Duran and Kajagoogoo would be the two biggest bands in the world. For a couple of exhilarating months this seemed a distinct possibility.

The record of 'Too Shy' came out perfectly. It seemed to me to be an inevitable smash. Not only was it suitable for both the UK and US charts, EMI had cunningly scheduled its release for early January. At this time of year the public was desperate for something fresh after a holiday period without new material, yet major artists were not likely to issue new releases, having put out their albums in the autumn to catch the holiday buying season. The act that made the first impression in January was likely to emerge as The Face of 1983.

I happened to have a new television series, *The Other Side of the Tracks*, beginning on Channel 4. As fate would have it – and fate certainly did seem to have something to do with it – the first programme was due to be transmitted on the Saturday evening preceding the Monday morning release of 'Too Shy'. I had already recorded a lengthy interview with Phil Collins that, fully illustrated, would take up the first two-thirds of the hour. Having the bulk of the show devoted to an artist who was a major star, I wanted to balance the programme with something fresh as a closer.

There is only one thing a music presenter likes better than to be right with one of his predictions and that is to be seen to be right. Knowing 'Too Shy' was a certain smash, I thought it would help the popular credibility of *The Other Side of the Tracks* to be indelibly associated with the debut of Kajagoogoo. Director Rod Taylor agreed with me that a feature on how a band is launched would be a perfect complement to our Phil Collins feature, and so we prepared the piece during the autumn of 1982.

In reality our show was the group's second TV appearance, but the first had been a low profile affair that didn't register in public memory. If I may say so, it also had not helped you overcome your jitters in front of the camera. I'm sure you remember your nervousness during our interview. Still, this was nothing compared to the edginess of Bryan Ferry in a subsequent edition of *The Other Side of the Tracks*, when he lit a cigarette and attempted to put it in his mouth only to discover he already had one there.

Between the time we filmed our launch of Kajagoogoo report in November 1982 and the time it was transmitted at the beginning of January 1983, we became good friends. You were brimming over with ambition and ideas, an approach I loved. I had ten years of first-hand familiarity with the music business, which made me a good guide for you on your travels into pop star territory. By the time 'Too Shy' started climbing the charts, we loved each other dearly.

And you loved clubbing. For you hardly a day was complete without a little visit to one of the clubs. As a measure of my commitment to you, which astonishes me even now, I went out with you to a club almost every night for most of 1983. This changed radically later in the year when I became one of the founder presenters on breakfast television, after which I went to bed earlier and earlier, but 1983 was certainly the Year of 1,000 Clubs – or at least the same clubs a thousand times. Often we visited two or three in an evening.

There was almost always the Gardens on Sunday night, Bang on Monday and Thursday, and Bolts on Friday.

Heaven was a must on Saturday and a fill-in some mid-week nights. Each had its own atmosphere.

I can recall having seen the New York Dolls in their London showcase at the Gardens club on the roof of a former department store in Kensington. Everyone always dressed properly there, it being Sunday night and flamingos watching from the little ponds outside. If it was warm, we could sit in one of the three themed gardens. If cold, there were areas inside reserved for sitting and talking – precious sane spaces rare in a nightclub. We would have a buffet dinner and then dance ourselves silly, violating all known medical advice against heavy exercise within an hour of a meal. It was a good thing we didn't try to swim in the ponds. The song I associate most with the Gardens is 'Flashdance . . . What a Feeling' by Irene Cara, from 'our year' of 1983.

I played 'Flashdance' for friends the other evening and unexpectedly became very emotional. Now emotion is not the first thing you would ordinarily associate with a Giorgio Moroder record. You should know, you made some! When I thought about it, I realized that 'Flashdance' was the last great twelve-inch I danced to with abandon, every week, before I learned about AIDS in June of 1983. As a matter of fact it was the American number one the very week I found out about the disease from my friend David in New York. When I hear 'Flashdance', I can feel the tremendous rush of excitement as dozens of beautiful young men pour on to the dance floor without care and without fear. And then I sense the dark curtain drawn, and the warning that we can never be that innocent again. We will have the same feeling of community, perhaps, with a heightened sense of shared experience, but it will be a community whose bonds are forged not only by pride but also by greater suffering and sacrifice than any of us could have imagined we would be expected to bear.

All of this is recalled by one record. Such is the power of music.

Bang was a far less formal place. It was the club with

the youngest regular clientele, late teens and young twenties being well represented. Favourite songs here included 'The Model' by Kraftwerk, 'Hit and Run Lover' by Carol Jiani and the twelve-inch of the Human League's 'Don't You Want Me'. I would be embarrassed if someone tabulated the number of conversations I abruptly terminated when I heard the first notes of 'Your Love' by Lime. I had to dance whenever I heard that record.

Holiest of holies was the full Disconet remix of 'Lay All Your Love on Me' by Abba. Like dogs responding to a high frequency whistle, we all descended on the dance floor the moment the first few chords were played. Abba may not have needed another number one – they had nine as it was – but they could have hit double figures if only they had released the Disconet version. When the record company realized it had a dance smash on its hands, it put out the album track as a single. How dumb! It peaked in the UK chart at seven. The Disconet mix was a number one that never was. We didn't care – it was our own private number one, and I can't count how many years gay people were dancing queens for 'Lay All Your Love On Me'. 'Dancing Queen' itself, of course, caught up with its subsequent revivals.

Bang had a less sexually threatening atmosphere than several other clubs. Several friendships we made there proved genuine and enduring. I'm struck at this moment by the memory of Graham Chapman, the writer and comic actor who was part of *Monty Python*. Although I was very much a junior celebrity compared to this good man, he nonetheless confided in me experiences that might not have been fully appreciated by his heterosexual colleagues. What an odd relationship we had – two men sharing sexual anecdotes in a spirit of camaraderie derived from both being gay public personalities.

He knew how to tell them. My favourite was the story of his trip to a northern town where, having to stay in a hotel for the night, Graham asked the bellboy if he knew of 'a club where one could find willing young men'. The bellboy sheepishly replied that he did not, and Graham went to bed.

In the middle of the night he was startled by someone opening the door of his room. He was even more startled when this stranger started climbing into his bed. It was the bellboy!

I miss the *rapport* I enjoyed with Graham. But I'm pleased to have the same sharing with other 'celebs', as you would call them. When two gay public personalities swap stories, there are no holds barred. Heaven knows the needle on the dishometer peaked whenever we gossiped. Remember the lead singer of a group also big in 1983 who, while pulling his trousers back up, told his lover, 'Remember, just because we've had sex doesn't mean I'm homosexual'? Or the Radio 1 DJ who told me he was going to get married for publicity and then two years later get divorced for even more publicity? We were often in stitches at the ludicrous extent to which our gay colleagues would go to pull the wool over the eyes of the wolfpack from Fleet Street. Perhaps the most hilarious was another lead singer of a number one group, a sweet effeminate man who claimed in a Sunday newspaper that he had enjoyed over a hundred female lovers.

Of course I have the greatest sympathy for these tortured souls. They clearly believed their careers would not survive if they were 'exposed' – the word 'outed' had not yet been popularized. Unlike Elton John, who had bravely discussed his sexuality openly, they did not feel their work was strong enough to survive the possible ending of their pin-up status with young girls. I certainly could not condemn a young man who thought his only shot at making his mark in the world might be destroyed by a lowlife from the tabloids.

It was a preposterous situation, of course. If the general public realized that about thirty per cent of show-business stars are gay, lesbian or bisexual, a great deal of prejudice would evaporate overnight. More importantly, more young people would have additional role models and would themselves be less afraid to 'come out', leading to a further reduction in ill will. There's nothing like having a friend or family member in a group previously considered mysterious to make that group seem conventional. Distinguishing between persons based on their sexual preference is an odd obsession of our time which has begun to and will continue to fade. I do believe that in my lifetime people will look back and wonder what all the fuss was about.

It was a popular assumption both in the tabloid press and the gay world that we were lovers. We, of course, knew we were not. Even more importantly we knew we were not going to become lovers. This is not to insult either of us, but rather to say that we could deal with the pressure because we had a precise idea of where we stood. Innuendo was not going to tempt us into either conforming to rumour or breaking up in exasperation.

As is so often the case with newspapers, the truth is perhaps more interesting than what is printed. We each had our own sex lives. Yours is your own to recall, although I would imagine you are unlikely to reminisce long over the odd phase you went through in which you were attracted to men with large noses. Do you remember? You believed that a big nose was evidence of overall physical endowment and dated a series of men based on the size of their proboscises. I can now tell you how angry I was with you when we spent a few days' vacation at my parents' place in Florida and you imported a friend from New York strictly on the size of his hooter.

I was not searching for a man with a trunk. I was, clichéd as it sounds, looking for love. Coming out of my three-and-a-half-year relationship with Stephen, I naively assumed that I would soon find a partner suitable for another three-and-a-half-year stint. But, in early 1983, before knowledge of AIDS swept the clubs, London's gay young things were more likely to want a one-night stand than an engagement.

I never went into a sexual situation anticipating a one-nighter because I couldn't bear it emotionally. Whereas many men seemed to want a good time followed by a good-bye, I was a romantic and became attached to those to whom I was attracted. I would never sleep with someone if I felt I might not do so again.

Being known publicly worked against me. Some people told me outright they couldn't bear the feeling that they were the junior partner in a relationship. Like Stephen, they believed that, if we were seen together, others would assume they had nothing to offer but, shall we say, youthful enthusiasm.

One young man, a clothes designer from East London named Michael, asked me one night in bed, 'If I were your boyfriend, would you pay for me to go to New York with you?'

'Of course,' I replied. 'My family live there.'

'I couldn't accept that,' he said. 'I have to pay my own way and right now I can't afford to fly to America. I don't think I should be your boyfriend.'

And so he wasn't. He became the lover of another man, who gave him HIV. After a remarkably quick series of illnesses, Michael died. He never had the chance to use his talents. Of course I have wondered if he would still be alive today if he had been able to be my lover, and naturally I have asked myself the same question about a couple of other young men I adored who chose another lifestyle and are now deceased. But, if I dwell on this variation of survivor guilt, I get nowhere. It doesn't bring my loved ones back, and it makes me depressed.

There were a number of other people with whom I made a false start during the year you and I were together. Some of them you missed when you were away doing concerts and promotional work. I can't even remember if you recall my enthusiasm the night I met someone at Heaven who looked very much like Stephen. I was walking through the Star Bar and there, standing by the wall and looking like he wanted company, was this near vision. He wasn't a dead ringer for my recent ex, but he was close enough for me to want to strike up a conversation.

He must have evoked in me feelings very similar to those Stephen brought out in my first meeting with him, because, as with Stephen, I broke my own rule against taking someone home on the first night. I just didn't want to miss the opportunity to begin a relationship that, I now realize, would have been merely an echo of my partnership with Stephen.

After our first loving night together the lookalike gave me his phone number and expressed the wish we meet again, as Stephen had done our first morning after. But my calls to the number, although always answered politely by a woman, were not returned. Finally, one day, my new friend phoned. He was crying.

'I've come to a phone box in the middle of some fields near home,' he told me, his voice shaking. 'I can't call you from the house.'

'What's the matter? Is there anything I can do?'

'No, there's nothing you can do, and I can't see you again. I mustn't.'

'Why not?' I protested. 'If you want to, we should.'

'I want to, but I mustn't. There's something I haven't told you.'

'What could be so important it would keep us apart if we wanted to be together?'

'I'm a prostitute. People pay me for sex. It's my job. I'm not good enough for you. Find someone else.'

'OK, I'm surprised,' I admitted, 'but you didn't ask me for money when we were together and you seemed very sincere.'

'I was sincere and that's the problem,' my friend cried. 'I want to be with you but, if I am, I don't want to be with people paying me, and that means I would have no job, and I want to work.'

The remaining two minutes of this excruciating

conversation consisted of variations on this theme. I am by no means saying that all prostitutes consider themselves 'not good enough' for somebody who doesn't pay them. The psychology of the rent boy is worth an entire book, but it's one I am not qualified to write. My brief encounter with the Stephen lookalike is all I have to go by. Excusing himself, he left my life, alone in the middle of a field, weeping. I never heard from him again.

Another possible romance never got beyond the first kiss stage. I had gone to my room with Laurence and just achieved mutual lip massage when I heard your keys turn in the front door.

'Who's that?' he cried out, alarmed.

'My housemate,' I answered casually.

'Limahl?' he asked in terror.

'Yes, what's wrong? He won't interrupt us.'

'I mustn't let him see me! I've got to leave, now!'

Unbelievably, the moment you entered your room, Laurence fled the house never to return. Now, Chris, what was that all about? At first I thought it was a heightened sensitivity to the presence of pop singers. A couple of years later I realized this could not possibly be the case, as Laurence had become the lover of another number one chart star.

That same year I got a bit beyond the kissing stage with another potential partner, a northerner named Edward. But, to what was then my discomfort and what became my deep regret, I could not accept his love. Edward was camp. He couldn't help it, he was really effeminate. One night he made an anguished phone call pleading with me to try having a relationship with him. He loved me and wanted to devote himself to me. I had pointed out accurately that we shared many interests, why couldn't we share each other?

I knew I was breaking Edward's heart, but I had to turn him down. I was not yet at the point where I could feel completely comfortable with a camp partner. Stephen had been a rugby player, for heaven's sake; Edward was just too – different. I was panicked by his overt queeniness. Despite his love and physical beauty, I had to disappoint him.

One of the lessons of Gay Liberation was that, if homosexuals wanted respect from the general population, they were required in turn to honour their own diverse groups. Straight-acting men just had to grit their teeth and accept that effeminate queens, who had given the world its stereotype of homosexuals, were equally real and equally worthy of respect. It is one of the measures of our progress in the last fifteen years that few of us now feel embarrassed by any of us. The gay community really did become that – a community, a melting pot of populations.

I don't know if today I would feel love for Edward as a potential partner. But I do know that, outside of times when I myself have been rejected, the greatest regrets I have about my romantic affairs are that in 1983 I hurt him and in 1984 lost touch with him. He is the person I wish I could see tonight and say, 'Listen, I'm really sorry.'

Although there was absolutely no evidence to suggest that you and I were lovers, I could understand why some people would want to believe it.

We were, after all, very loving towards each other. One evening in Palm Beach we went out to dinner and you staggered me by saying, 'I think the reason we're so close is we must've known each other in a previous life.' I wasn't so sure I agreed, but I was flattered that you'd taken the time to think about it.

The idea of two persons in the public eye enjoying each other in private appeals to the prurient in all of us. I recall how, at the same time as our alleged romance, one of my group and one of your circle were supposedly having an affair – that is, a DJ and a member of a top teen group. Both of these unfairly handsome young men went on to marry, which is in itself no proof of heterosexuality. Arranged marriages can be the last refuge of the confused and the craven, but this doesn't mean that everyone who gets married is concealing desires for members of the same sex. I knew the rumour about our two friends was false. Drat! It was too horny not to be true, but untrue it was.

An even more bizarre pairing was suggested by my friend Lol Creme of 10C.C.. Backstage at a Roxy Music concert, he could no longer contain his curiosity.

'Paul, excuse me for asking this,' he said, turning untypically formal. 'I know it's none of my business, but I've heard a rumour that's so strange I have to ask you about it.'

'Go ahead,' I replied, 'it can't be any stranger than others I've heard.'

It was. Lol had been told that a Radio 1 DJ had developed a close personal friendship with a politician. Needless to say, both were men.

I happen to know how this rumour started, because I had introduced the two people in question. At a reception to honour Paul McCartney, Tim Rice had introduced me to the politician.

'There's no need for explanations,' the politician interrupted. 'I'm a regular listener to Paul's programme. And I'm a great fan of one of his colleagues.'

I assumed he was referring to the Radio 4 arts review programme *Kaleidoscope*, on which I often appeared. But who could the colleague be? Perhaps one of the *Today* presenters? A news reader?

When he named one of the cute young Radio 1 recruits, my jaw almost hit the floor.

'You must arrange for us to meet at lunch,' he added.

I thought he was being rhetorical, like every false friend in Los Angeles who closes conversations by saying, 'Let's do lunch,' but he actually meant it. McCartney received his prize, Wayne Sleep was introduced as the man who had performed the most twirls in mid-air, and Tim and I met the man who had survived the fastest deceleration in history. His racing car had hit a wall, an incident he shrugged off by saying, 'My balls really hurt for a while, that's all.' Then I started to leave the room.

'Don't forget our lunch!' cried the politician, and I knew I was going to book for three at Langan's. This public meal, at which the politician doled out the sauté potatoes like mother, must have caught the attention of rumour-mongers. Radio 1 DJs of the time loved publicity, but not scandal, and none that I knew would entertain the idea of an affair with a politician. There was never any indication the man wanted a sexual relationship either.

'So you see, Lol,' I concluded, 'there's no truth to the rumour. Who asked you about it?'

Creme paused for a moment and then replied, 'Eric Clapton.'

Eric Clapton? How did he get into it? When even the god of guitarists could get involved in the spreading of a rumour, I knew there was no resisting the virus-like infection of tantalizing suggestion.

So it was with you and I. More than a few celebrity-watchers entertained sordid fantasies about what happened in our house when the lights went out. What happened was sleep, but sleep does not sell papers.

A German magazine had a photographer hide behind the stone wall of the church across the road from our house and take pictures whenever we went in or out together. The rag – er, mag – finally ran a two-page spread. On one page you were in the company of a young woman, on the facing page you were with me. Large question marks were superimposed on the woman and myself. I don't read German, but I didn't need to to understand the meaning of 'homosexuelle DJ Paul Gambaccini'.

Idiotic pieces ran regularly in the *Sun*. After Kajagoogoo dropped you, Nick Beggs was infuriated that the paper's pop columnist claimed he'd voted to sack you after having a vision of an angel. 'That was just totally made up, absolute rubbish!' he told *Melody Maker*. Nick joined us at being enraged at the female *Sun* writer who claimed the group broke up because it found our friendship embarrassing.

'This is a very important point,' Nick told the MM. 'The fact that Limahl had a relationship of any sort with Paul had nothing whatsoever to do with our decision. I still regard Paul as a very good friend . . . '

And *vice versa*. Chris, you should know that I still use the radio alarm clock Kajagoogoo gave me for my birthday in 1983. I have only pleasant associations with this generous gift, which was presented before the band had received any royalties at all.

We have to shrug. The tabloids and pop papers in this country go on a new feeding frenzy every edition. We were in the public eye and happened to be worth a meal or two. But that shouldn't mean the writing has to be wildly inaccurate, as it was in the case of the *Sun*, or rude, as in the example of Julie Burchill.

'As screambait Kajagoogoo make good fagbait,' she wrote in her 'review' of your *White Feathers* album, 'totally lacking the clean sheen of Duran Duran. The singer looks like the resident rodent in a Leicester Square lavatory,' and so on. Nice musical analysis, Julie! The pleasure which this journalist took in gratuitously insulting you, Chris, enabled me to enjoy guilt-free laughter when the shoe was on the other foot. A famous comedian, reversing the anti-fur protest slogan, referred to her as an example of 'cruelty without beauty'.

If the greatest revenge is to be good to your oppressor then I have enjoyed tremendous vengeance on Rick Sky, the *Star*'s pop columnist when the band let you go. I returned home that day and, to my complete astonishment, found Rick Sky sitting in the living-room. This is not the sort of greeting a working man wants on coming back to his house. He was next to you on the sofa, pumping you with questions about the group.

'Don't worry,' you attempted to reassure me, 'it's all right. Rick says he won't write a story unless he turns on the tape recorder, and he won't do that unless we give him permission.'

We never gave him permission, he never turned on the tape recorder and a huge story and photograph appeared in the next day's *Star*.

'I was sacked says Limahl' read the headline, next to a picture of you at the front door of the house. 'By RICK SKY', read the by-line, 'ANOTHER STAR EXCLUSIVE'.

Major lowlife, I thought, major lowlife. A few years later, when he had changed employers, I got back at him by doing him a massive favour. There is nothing more humiliating than putting someone who has wronged you into your debt. At a London party for Whitney Houston, the manager of another of rock's greatest stars, having taken offence at Sky's recent comments about his charge, took Rick by the lapels, held him against a pillar and started banging his head against it. Fortunately, the manager, one of my friends, was considerably the worse for wear and wasn't strong enough to do immediate injury, but the situation was serious. A few more blows of any force and Sky's skull could have been damaged.

'You don't want to do that, John,' I said gently, dissuading the manager from further expressing his temper. Sky slinked off without so much as a thank you and didn't give me credit for saving his skin in his front-page account of the incident in the next day's *Sun*. When I questioned him about this curious omission, he explained he had been too shocked to notice the identity of his rescuer.

We never knew when harrassment would next occur. One day I was telephoned at Radio 1 in the middle of the afternoon by a reporter from the *News of the World*. He advised me that I should see him for my own good, and that I should see him immediately. Of course I recognized this as a threat and tried to prepare myself psychologically for an inquisition from this notorious publication. I kept in mind the experience of a female friend, a TV performer who had recently granted an interview and been horrified to read a story concentrating almost exclusively on her sex life and large breasts. I could have warned her that, with this newspaper, it was feel ya, not Ophelia, that was of interest.

I arranged with my accuser to meet at Patisserie Valerie in Old Compton Street. If I was going to be subjected to sordid suggestions, I might as well get a decent hot chocolate out of it. Only a couple of sips in, the personal questions started.

During the ten-minute walk from Broadcasting House to Soho I had steeled myself against giving anything away. Here was the one occasion I can recall when I did not freely discuss my sexuality.

'You are homosexual, aren't you, Paul?' I was grilled by Mr Grub. 'You can tell me that, can't you?'

'I'm sure my lawyer will find this conversation interesting,' I replied. I knew I had to give lateral responses, not a yes or a no. 'Yes' and he had a story; 'no' and he had a denial, which was in itself a story.

The reason I was going along with this meeting was that I knew Grub must have some fantastic tale to tell. There must have been a rumour floating around Fleet Street or a member of the public trying to sell a story about my sex life. I had to be informed about any efforts to discredit me.

'We have on tape a conversation with a teenager called David,' the reporter got to the heart of the matter. 'He is sixteen years old,' Grub continued. 'This makes him a minor. Have you ever had sex with an underage male?'

'What an interesting conversation,' I replied.

'Being gay is one thing, Paul, I can understand that. But sex with a minor is against the law. That is a criminal offence.'

Duh, I thought. Something against the law is a criminal offence! This guy should be teaching Tautology 101 . . .

'Have you, Paul? Have you?'

'What does David say?' I had to find out if David was

accusing me of underage sex. But no. Guess what, Chris! He was accusing me of having sex with you!

'David says he went to your birthday party and you had sex with Limahl on the kitchen floor in front of the guests.'

This was the big one, I thought, the big lie every gay celebrity waits for. Print this whopper and you print my pension! I'll see you in court and . . .

'My lawyer will find that very interesting,' I said.

'He says he met Boy George at the party.'

Now I understood what had happened. All Radio 1 DJs wound up with multiple promotional copies of certain LPs. I made a point of giving away most of the extras, often at personal appearances. I had met young David, a Boy George fan, and given him a duplicate copy of the album *Kissing To Be Clever* by George's group Culture Club. From receiving the record he had fantasized I had actually introduced him to his hero. He had invented the sex story since he had heard you and I were lovers.

'Boy George has never been to my flat,' I honestly declared. 'I don't think you have a story.'

'Then you should know that David's boyfriend is going around Fleet Street with a tape of David's accusations.'

And so he had. The teenager's older boyfriend, upon learning of his lover's acquaintance with me, had decided to act as his agent and take his recorded story with its foul fictions around the tabloids. Another paper almost bit, but the *News of the World* was the only one that actually sent a reporter after me.

'Believe me,' I told Grub, 'you're wasting your time. And I've got to get back to work.'

I reached for some money to pay for my hot chocolate, but he insisted on paying.

'I'm sorry, Paul,' he said sadly, as if he were the one suddenly seeking comfort. 'I'm just doing my job.'

'I wonder,' I speculated as we left the patisserie, 'if, when you were a boy, you wanted to be a journalist when you grew up.'

Grub winced.

'Ask yourself what happened along the way. Oh, and by the way,' I pointed to beneath his overcoat, 'is that where you keep the tape recorder?'

'Paul, don't say that.'

Of course, I had no idea whether he had taped our conversation or not, but I had to assume it was a possibility. I never saw or heard from Grub again.

I was occasionally warned that one tabloid in particular was gunning for me. A female editor had 'Gambaccini sex scandal' on her running-list of possible features, but could never find any scandal. Male prostitutes retained by the newspaper as sexual equivalents of stringers were paid to inform the editor if any public personalities, including myself, ever hired a rent boy. Since I have never paid for sex in my life, I wasn't particularly worried about that one. But I mean, really, don't these people have something better to do with their time, like pick their noses or fart?

I'm sure you remember your own close encounter with the *News of the World*. The main reason you wanted to move in with me after the success of 'Too Shy', other than the fact we were getting on famously, was that you felt you were living on the edge of a front-page story waiting to be reported. The son of a parliamentary figure, your landlord required an exotic form of stimulation from strangers to achieve satisfaction. You knew from the comings and goings in the house that this sideshow would inevitably be reported by Fleet Street. The public had a seemingly insatiable desire for reading about even the most tenuous links between the Establishment and sexual unorthodoxy.

On two consecutive Saturday evenings we drove to open-air news stands where Sunday papers were sold early to see if your unfortunate acquaintance had been exposed. We both knew that, in the logic of these things, both the parliamentary officer, being his father, and you, being his celebrity lodger, would be on the front page with him even though neither of you had anything to do with his intriguing search for pleasure. I'll admit this Saturday night cruising of Marble Arch and King's Cross was my idea, as I had recently discovered it was the best way of learning the *Sunday Times* chart positions of *The Guinness Book of British Hit Singles* a few hours early.

Fortunately, there was no Sunday headline linking you with this man while you lived in his house. Nor, for that matter, while you lived in mine. It was only some time later that, sure enough, the story ran on the front page of the *News of the World* with a headline mentioning the parliamentary officer and a photograph showing you with your landlord.

Chris, would you believe that, when I applied to college in 1966, I put down my likely career as 'journalist'? I cannot think of a profession which has taken a bigger swan dive in my estimation during my lifetime than tabloid reporter. It isn't just that these people dine on celebrity excrement for a living. They actually aspire to eat our shit.

I'm so proud that, despite all the preposterous attention, we carried on with our friendship. One way I knew we were unusually close was that it felt natural driving you in my car. That may sound an odd indicator of friendship levels, so let me explain. In the music business one inevitably gives lifts to people from all aspects of the profession, from disc jockeys to promotion men to artists. With the exception of yourself, I was always conscious when ferrying a performer from place to place that I was carrying precious cargo. With memories of Buddy Holly in mind, I was always aware of the need to drive carefully. When driving Bob Geldof and Paula Yates, for example, I would be aware that one close encounter with a stray telegraph pole and there would be no more performances of 'Rat Trap'. (Nor, for that matter, would there have been Live Aid a few years later. Can you imagine the retrospective headline on God's Daily News: 'Millions Starve in 1985 Because Gambaccini Was Crap Driver in 1980'?)

Two particular instances of having number one artists

in my car remain vivid. The first concerns the artist formerly known as Garfunkel, who preferred to be called Arthur when we were mutual dining companions of the singer-songwriter Stephen Bishop at a Chinese restaurant in Chelsea. This was when the extremely talented Stephen seemed to have the aristocracy of popular music at his beck and call. How he managed to get Eric Clapton and Chaka Khan to perform on his debut album I'll never know. Garfunkel gave Bishop's 'Looking for the Right One' a beautiful reading on his own 1975 album *Breakaway*, which included his British number one single 'I Only Have Eyes for You.'

Upon arriving at the restaurant, I was introduced to Arthur and an actress. I will exercise some discretion here, Chris, not only to show you that I occasionally can but also because this pleasant woman did not go on to have a happy life. But that evening she was bubbling, greeting me enthusiastically.

'Why, Paul, it's good to see you again!' she gushed.

It was certainly good to see someone of her charm and friendliness, but the 'again' bit escaped me.

'Good to see you,' I replied.

After the first course, she struck a look of bewilderment. 'How long has it been, Paul?' she asked.

'A couple of years,' I answered. If we had met, this would certainly have been true.

After the main course she not only reached for her napkin but also threw in the towel.

'Where did we first meet, Paul?' she enquired frustratedly.

'At a *Rolling Stone* party,' I said, doing some quick lateral thinking. In those days *Rolling Stone* magazine did have the odd party or two and, if we had indeed met, which I was now beginning to think was less likely than having met Mao, it would have been in New York at a *Stone* soirée.

'Of course,' she smiled, indicating that, as I had guessed, she had at least once been a guest of our beloved boss Jann Wenner.

Ever the gentleman, Garfunkel at no time attempted to dominate the conversation and only obliquely referred to his historic partnership with Paul Simon by using the expression 'the success'. At the time of our dinner he was particularly pleased that he had taken time to do some walking in Asia, which I guess answers the question what does a man do after he's sold tens of millions of records and acted with Jack Nicholson?

When the dinner was over and everyone had given their thanks to our host Stephen Bishop – had he ever taken Clapton and Chaka for a Chinese, I briefly wondered? – I left and got into my car, which I had parked right outside the restaurant. Before setting off I looked into my rear-view mirror and there, to my astonishment, was Garfunkel, sitting perfectly still in the back seat, almost meditating.

'Arthur,' I tried to keep my cool, 'are you all right?'

'Oh, hello, Paul,' he said.

Paul and Arthur! This was the closest I ever got to Gambaccini and Garfunkel.

'Can I give you a lift somewhere?'

I don't know how chauffeurs can take the tension – I couldn't bear having the future of 'Bridge Over Troubled Water' sitting in my back seat – but I was at least determined to be helpful.

'Oh, no, I just thought this was my ride. I'll go look for my driver. Thanks, Paul.'

And those were the last words that polite gentleman ever said to me. Upon reflection, I couldn't help but wonder how he ever thought my little Fiat was his limousine, but I never question the judgment of a supreme talent. Well, almost never. If he had asked, I would have advised him against appearing in *Boxing Helena*.

The other number one artist whose trip in my car is indelibly etched in my memory must remain anonymous. I was driving around Hyde Park Corner when he yelled, 'Stop! Pull over!'

'How can I pull over? This is Hyde Park Corner!' I shouted back.

'Go on that side road. I see a cottage!'

True enough, this teen idol had spied a men's lavatory near the Underground station and instructed me to enter the park so he could go and cruise the toilet. I needed a nap anyway, so I drove into Hyde Park, stopped at the side of the road and slept for twenty minutes while our mutual friend went looking for love. He returned unfulfilled, but I was refreshed.

Cottaging is a minority activity that gets the attention of the majority by its sheer audacity. To me its appeal is as unfathomable as that of smoking, but a lot of people smoke and some people go cottaging. So, even if our number one pop star wanted to run a number of risks for what for me would be incomplete satisfaction, I shrugged my shoulders and just hoped he didn't encounter a wrong partner, a policeman or a reporter, just as I shrugged those same shoulders when my brother became a leading executive of a cigarette company. I merely hope he doesn't smoke too many.

Inevitably, for us, there came the last lift. Why, at the end of 1983, did you leave my house? Why did we no longer hang out together wherever queens of quality gathered?

You became your own man. As royalties started to come in, you formed your own economic unit. You bought a flat, in which you conducted your own love life. You no longer needed me to supply you with security or reassurance.

I choose the word 'security' advisedly. Many relationships between gay men ten or more years apart become intense when an insecure younger party turns to the older one for security. The latter is only too glad to oblige. After all, he has, with rare exception, no gay little brothers nor children of his own, and to be able to offer a sense of safety and self-worth to a younger person is a great and pleasant privilege.

This most intimate variety of relationship is, to use one of your favourite words, doomed. If successful, the younger person develops his feeling of self-worth and no longer needs the older man for security. A comes to B for security. B gives it. A goes. That's life.

But after the pain, after the sense of loss, must come a feeling of immense personal achievement. After 1983 I 'never' saw you – meaning that our contact was limited to a few times a year. But I had to be happy for you. You no longer needed me or anyone like me. You no longer needed to call me from some hotel in Europe, afraid that someone was going to beat you up, or go shopping with you in Carnaby Street because you were afraid mods were going to do you damage. You weren't afraid that anybody was going to harm you any more. If I kept you secure while you developed that sense of safety, I made a worthwhile contribution to your life.

The early 1980s are now long gone. The era in which Kajagoogoo existed has even been the subject of nostalgic celebrations in clubs and on cable channels. People assume that entertainers have peaked when their moment of highest professional visibility is past. It won't surprise you to hear that several people on occasion have asked what you are now doing, as if your interest in music necessarily terminated the moment Limahl left the charts.

I tell this story to show how popular success is as ephemeral to the people who experience it as to those who observe it. In 1995 Marco Pierre White opened his Criterion Restaurant at Piccadilly Circus. He was taking over from Bob Payton, my old restaurateur friend who had died suddenly behind the wheel. That someone larger than life could no longer be in it was unacceptable and reminded us all that it isn't just AIDS which kills people. Human beings continue to die from all the other causes that ever nailed them; it's just we've grown so accustomed to AIDS deaths that it almost surprises us when someone boards the train to nowhere for another reason.

Marco offered me a table on his first night. I accepted his gracious invitation and filled it with friends I thought would enjoy each other's company. Besides Tony Vickers, who was working for me at the time, I invited you, Terry's survivor Rob Kean, Radio 3 broadcaster Richard Coles, and the writer and television presenter Howard Schuman. I enjoyed the greatest thrill any host can have – to see his guests get along famously. Only when our group had left the restaurant and some of us had dived into Piccadilly Circus tube did it hit me.

'Howard!' I cried, stopping in my tracks. 'Do you know what I didn't realize until now?'

'No,' my old friend replied. (Strange, isn't it, Chris, how a man of words like Howard only winds up with one two-letter word in this epistle?)

'With the exception of Tony, who is getting into production with Rob and would like to have one, all of you have had number one records – Chris with Kajagoogoo, you with *Rock Follies*, Richard with the Communards, and Rob as co-writer/producer with East 17. And yet none of you at any part of the evening talked about having had a number one record. That, I submit, is how important having a number one is in the personal lives of those who have them!'

It had to be true. None of you reminisced about *Top of the Pops*. All of you spoke with enthusiasm about current and future projects. I find this inspiring in my own career, Chris. I can't say I've had an identifiable single high point yet since I've never peaked, but the knowledge that you can leave the papers and the media behind, and actually get on with things is a tremendous relief. When I was a boy, a daytime disc jockey in New York also enjoyed success as a night-time novelty character named Mad Daddy. His creation proved more popular than his own person. When he lost his own show, he took his life. This was, at least, how I read the story of his death when I was a schoolboy, and this interpretation made a deep impression on me.

When I began working in radio, I made a mental note to myself never to take my career as seriously as Mad Daddy.

To know that you and Howard and Richard could enjoy and then surrender the number one position without trauma is a great relief to me. You are living proof that when one door closes, another really does open.

People affect the lives of those in their orbit even after they stop thinking they have an influence, and I can cite two major ways in which you affect my life every day. The first is in my domestic eating habits. You were a vegetarian. Since we had many meals together, this led to my gradually cutting out red meat. Cheeseburgers from Joe Allen and Ed's were the last to go, since these places had the best restaurant and diner burgers, respectively, in London. Even when you moved out of the house I didn't go back to eating meat. I found it fatty and heavy. In these circumstances the weight of moral arguments against meat-eating took on decisive force. Gradually I ceased eating chicken, and then fish, at home. This would please Linda McCartney, whose first or second remark every time I saw her was, 'Are you veggie yet?'

The second and most profound way you affected my life in the long term is through the house I live in. During early 1983 I was looking for a house to buy in Blackheath and Notting Hill Gate, then my two favourite parts of London. I could find nothing in my price range I really wanted. I knew that, when it came to something as important as a house, I had to be in love with the place from the moment I saw it.

One evening we were eating at your favourite restaurant, Manna, in Primrose Hill. By this time I had been looking in Blackheath and Notting Hill Gate for two months, and was reduced to peering in every estate agent's window, regardless of which part of town I was in. As we came out of Manna I noticed an estate agent up the road. I asked if you minded if I had a peek. You didn't, and we looked at the offerings. One of the properties was marked down a quarter, right into my price range, and sounded good. It was only a mile and a half away, so I proposed an instant reconnoitre. You came with me.

The house was fronted by cherry trees, which were in full pink bloom. An arch of beautiful blossom topped the entrance gate.

'If this place isn't a dump,' I said, 'I'm having it.' Thirteen years later I'm still 'having it' and I'm still loving it. And Chris, as I write this, the cherry trees are in bloom. Thanks for allowing me to check out the estate agent's window, and then the house that spring evening in 1983. It's appropriate that you yourself came to live here, if only for half a year. You may remember that we called it 'Pillars', after the preposterous one-word subhead in the *Evening Standard* report of our co-residence.

There is also a way in which you have inspired me recently, even in your physical absence. When we met, I had lived with Stephen for three years. You were unlikely to settle down with anyone for some time. Indeed, your personality and career were so tumultuous it was difficult to imagine you ever having a stable domestic life. As I write this, it is you who have lived with a man of your dreams for three years, and I who seem far from that goal. It is precisely because you have a happy home life that I now 'never' see you – two or three times a year instead of two or three times a week.

Of course, between the minute I send this and the moment you receive it the two of you may have an explosive argument over the best method of preparing vegetables and you might separate, but that seems unlikely. The point is that you have so far managed three years when none seemed imminent. I now look forward to that stability in my life. Thank you, Chris, not only for the memories but also for the inspiration. Despite all the factors that invite me to reflect on the past, your example helps me look in the only direction in which I can fruitfully travel – ahead.